Personnel Savings in Competitively Sourced DoD Activities

Are They Real?
Will They Last?

Susan M. Gates
Albert A. Robbert

Prepared for the Office of the Secretary of Defense

National Defense Research Institute

RAND

Competitive sourcing is currently viewed by the Office of the Secretary of Defense (OSD) as a means to reduce DoD infrastructure costs significantly and free up funds for other needs. Since infrastructure costs derive predominantly from labor, much of the expected savings will be related to reductions in the cost of personnel. At the request of the Office of the Deputy Assistant Secretary of Defense for Civilian Personnel Policy, RAND undertook a study to examine how competitive sourcing affects labor and other costs. Understanding more precisely how competitive sourcing lowers costs could contribute to better selection of activities to competitively source or other improvements in the competitive-sourcing process. It might also suggest efficiencies that can be exported to activities not subject to competitive sourcing.

This study's findings should be of interest to OSD, service, and defense agency managers and policymakers responsible for civilian personnel, manpower/resource management, competitive sourcing, and other related processes.

This research was conducted for the Deputy Assistant Secretary of Defense for Civilian Personnel Policy within the Forces and Resources Policy Center of RAND's National Defense Research Institute, a federally funded research and development center sponsored by the Office of the Secretary of Defense, the Joint Staff, the Unified Commands, and the defense agencies.

CONTENTS

FIGURES

ings has renewed interest in the A-76 process. The services plan to have examined over 200,000 positions in A-76 competititions between FY 1997 and 2005, a process that they expect will generate about $9 billion in savings. The services have programmed some of these anticipated savings into their budget submission.

This increased focus on A-76 studies as a means of generating cost savings raises significant issues for policymakers. In particular, it is important to understand the level of savings generated by the process over the long run, and to understand how those savings are achieved. The number of competitions will be limited by the resources available in the services and agencies to support competitions, and by the fact that inherently governmental activities are exempt from competitions. It might be possible to apply lessons learned to activities that will not be studied in an A-76 competition.

To assist DoD civilian personnel managers in addressing these concerns, we examined the implementation of six recent A-76 competitions and focused on the following questions:

- How large are the projected savings generated by these competitions?

- How were the projected cost savings achieved?

- Are the savings real and enduring?

- Could similar savings be achieved outside of the A-76 process?

Three of the competitions we examined were won by the in-house organization, and three were won by the contractor. The case study analysis consisted of document review, semistructured interviews, and an analysis of information derived from the documents and interviews.

FINDINGS

We found that the projected personnel cost savings are substantial in both in-house and contractor wins, ranging from 30 to 60 percent. In both in-house and contractor wins, projected savings stem largely from using fewer people to do the job. Less important strategies are downgrading positions and capital-labor substitution. In one case, the contractor expected to reduce costs by paying slightly lower wages, but this was not a significant or consistent source of savings in the competitions we examined.

In order to perform the work with fewer people, both contractors and in-house managers employed various labor-saving techniques: civilianization, organizational restructuring, multiskilling, reduced work scope, and increased labor availability. With the exception of increased labor availability, all of these labor-saving techniques appeared to be available to both the in-house and contractor organizations.

Examining the implementation of A-76 study results over periods ranging from one to ten years, we found that the anticipated personnel cost savings were generally realized and maintained over time. In particular, we found no clear and convincing evidence of cost increases over time in either in-house or contractor wins. However, we note the difficulty of disentangling the effects of mission change from those of pure cost escalation or decrease.

There are significant limitations with the cost data that are collected before, during, and after an A-76 study. These limitations make it difficult to evaluate whether the personnel cost savings generated by a particular activity examined in an A-76 competition lead to real savings for the DoD budget. We were able to identify several costs incurred by DoD in the course of the A-76 process that are unaccounted for in the data. We believe that DoD should find better ways of tracking (at least roughly) the relationship between mission and cost. In addition, in the case of MEO wins, DoD needs to track the costs, not merely the manpower authorizations, of in-house organizations.

Our interviews suggest that DoD would not find it easy to apply lessons learned from A-76 studies to improve the productivity of the government workforce. Managers face an incentive structure that deters them from making efficiency-enhancing changes. Managers tend to prefer current ways of doing business to voluntary cost-cutting activities. However, the A-76 process changes the manager's choice set so that the status quo is not an option.

CONCLUSIONS AND RECOMMENDATIONS

Improving Efficiency in Government Organizations

Several reforms to DoD's internal management system would be required to generate personnel cost savings outside of the A-76 process. First, the Office of the Secretary of Defense (OSD), Military Departments, and Defense Agencies need to provide more positive incentives to local commanders and managers to undertake such reforms. Both individual and organizational rewards could be used. Second, DoD needs to eliminate or reduce negative incentives to efficiency-enhancing changes, such as arbitrary budget cuts imposed on installations and staffing policies. While it is crucial to provide managers with positive incentives for change and to remove negative incentives, it is also important that front-line managers receive training and support that will enable them to undertake such reforms. Documenting and disseminating information on cost-saving initiatives throughout DoD may be important but cannot replace broader training of functional managers.

Data Needs for High-Level Decision Making

Consistent, high-quality information on cost savings and other outcomes of the A-76 process will allow OSD, Military Departments, and Defense Agencies to make better decisions about the future implementation of the process—the kind of savings they can expect, the time frame during which savings can be expected, and the activities they should target for A-76 competitions in the future.

Better information requires precise definitions of terms like "baseline cost" and "cost savings" that are consistent across installations and services. The development of these definitions must include consideration of whether they capture the total cost of an activity to the DoD. DoD might incur costs that are not captured in activity-level costing exercises.

In addition, the government must gather information on the cost of conducting the studies and continue to collect cost information during the implementation phase of the winning contract or MEO.

New Approaches to Managing the MEO

In the case of MEO wins, DoD should think about the procedures in place for managing the MEO. It is telling that the managers of MEO wins could not provide us with cost information—only information on authorized positions. DoD should consider giving MEO managers the tools to monitor and manage costs as well as freedom from constraints on the number and grade level of authorizations.

A large and growing community of researchers within RAND and the Center for Naval Analyses is interested in DoD competitive sourcing. We have benefited greatly from both formal and informal opportunities to exchange ideas with them. We thank Sue Hosek for the guidance she provided as director of the program under which this report was produced. RAND colleagues Laura Baldwin and Carole Roan Gresenz provided helpful reviews of an earlier draft. We also benefited from comments of seminar participants at the 1999 Western Economics Association Conference and from comments by Carla Tighe on earlier versions of this report. Gordon Lee, our communications analyst, helped us improve the clarity of the document. Lisa Hochman provided helpful secretarial support. Ron Key carefully edited the final copy.

Dr. Diane Disney, the Deputy Assistant Secretary of Defense for Civilian Personnel policy, and Dr. Larry Lacy, of DoD's Civilian Personnel Management Service, provided useful feedback on the research leading up to this report and on its previous versions.

Points of contact for the A-76 program at each service's headquarters and at several major commands and local installations were valuable sources of information and assistance—particularly Jim Wakefield of the Army's Office of the Assistant Chief of Staff for Installation Management, Annie Andrews of the Air Force's Directorate of Manpower, Organizations and Quality, and CDR (Sel) Steve Smith and LCDR Steve Gillespie at OPNAV N471F. They were instrumental in arranging the visits through which we developed the case studies in this report.

FY	fiscal year
FYDP	Future Years Defense Program
GAO	U.S. General Accounting Office
GS	General Schedule
IG	Inspector General
MEO	most efficient organization
MM	missile maintenance
MWR	morale, welfare, and recreation
NAF	nonappropriated fund
OMB	U.S. Office of Management and Budget
OPM	U.S. Office of Personnel Management
PPP	Priority Placement Program
PWS	performance work statement
QAE	quality assurance evaluator
RIF	reduction in force
RX	reparable exchange
SBA	Small Business Administration
SCA	Service Contract Act
TEL	Telecommunications operations and maintenance
WG	Wage Grade
WL	Wage Leader
WS	Wage Supervisor

Chapter One

INTRODUCTION

BACKGROUND

The Department of Defense (DoD) is under substantial pressure to manage its resources more effectively in order to free resources that can be used to fund weapon system modernization and quality of life improvements. Its strategy for accomplishing this reallocation has several components, including efforts to establish priorities and to improve efficiency. Core defense functions, which include intelligence, strategic defense, applied research and development, and the provision of operational forces, assume the highest priority. To perform these core functions, DoD must rely on a support infrastructure—a set of activities that are not directly part of the defense mission, but facilitate the realization of that mission.[1] As illustrated in Figure 1.1, approximately 60 percent of DoD's 1997 obligation authority funded infrastructure activities.[2] Personnel costs account for at least half of those infrastructure costs. Because these activities consume such a large proportion of the defense budget and are less directly related to the defense mission, they have become a natural focus of DoD cost-cutting efforts.

---

[1]DoD's 1993 Report on the Bottom-Up Review identified seven categories of infrastructure: logistics, medical, personnel, training, acquisition management, installation support, and force management.

[2]Infrastructure is not a formal DoD budget category, and hence these estimates are approximate. See GAO/NSIAD-96-176 for a discussion of infrastructure costs.

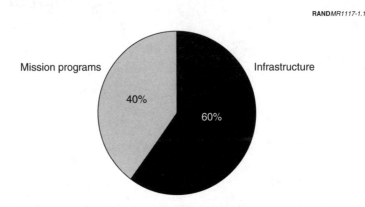

RAND*MR1117-1.1*

Figure 1.1—DoD Obligation Authority (1997)

By reducing costs in infrastructure areas, DoD hopes to limit the impact of budget cuts on directly mission-related activities.[3] DoD has identified competitive sourcing as one of the most promising avenues for reducing these infrastructure costs.[4]

Competitive Sourcing in DoD

Competitive sourcing is a general term describing a process through which managers consider both internal and external service providers to determine who can provide a given level of service at the

---

[3]Indeed, the 1996 Future Years Defense Program (FYDP) reflected a reduction of approximately 25 percent in infrastructure expenditure. However, GAO/NSIAD-98-204 argues that these anticipated reductions were exaggerated and they have been revised downward in the 1997 and 1998 FYDP.

[4]Other potentially important sources of infrastructure savings include large-scale restructuring of activities such as base closures and realignments, reductions in military construction costs, and process reengineering. See GAO/NSIAD-96-131 for a discussion of potential savings opportunities for DoD in the infrastructure area.

lowest cost.[5] Potential service providers include government employees within the organization (in-house providers), government employees in another organization (inter-service support providers), and private contractors.

It is important to distinguish the term *competitive sourcing* from the term *outsourcing*. Outsourcing refers to a process through which the provision of a service is contracted out to the most efficient external service provider. From the perspective of a government organization, an external provider may be either a private-sector entity or another government organization. Competitive sourcing, on the other hand, also considers how efficiently the in-house provider can provide the service. In other words, outsourcing is a more restrictive type of competitive sourcing that does not directly consider the possibility of in-house provision.

The federal government makes a distinction between activities that are inherently governmental and those that are commercial. Inherently governmental activities are "so intimately related to the public interest as to mandate performance by Federal employees."[6] So long as they are classified as such, inherently governmental activities cannot be contracted to an external private-sector provider. Inherently governmental activities involve policy determination or the direction and control of government resources (including federal employees).[7] Activities not inherently governmental are considered commercial.

Commercial activities are subject to a series of rules and procedures set forth in U.S. Office of Management and Budget (OMB) Circular A-76.[8] Every five years the A-76 program requires all government

---

[5]Competitive sourcing could also refer to the purchase of a good, but the current policy debate as well as this paper focuses on the acquisition of services.

[6]OMB Circular No. A-76—Revised Supplemental Handbook (March 1996), p. 36.

[7]A complete description of functions considered to be inherently governmental can be found in OMB Circular No. A-76—Revised Supplemental Handbook (March 1996), Appendix 5.

[8]The term "A-76" is often used as an adjective to describe rules, procedures, and processes related to the circular. The A-76 process attempts to balance the interests of the private sector (which believes that the government should not compete with its citizens) with those of federal employees (who believe they have a right to keep their jobs

agencies, including the DoD, to review commercial functions being performed in-house. Agencies can, however, exempt functions from the review process for reasons listed in OMB Circular A-76.[9] For example, the function may be exempt if it is critical to the national defense, involves the provision of health services to government employees, or if there is no private sector provider for the service.

At the beginning of this review process, the government must develop a formal document called the performance work statement (PWS) that describes, from a customer perspective, the work required. Ideally, the PWS describes the required output and level or quality of service, rather than the manner in which the service is to be provided.[10]

The PWS forms the basis of a competitive-bidding process through which the government compares potential private sector providers with the in-house provider. The in-house provider as well as the hopeful external providers submit detailed plans describing how they will accomplish tasks described in the PWS, along with an estimate of the cost of doing so. The bids are supposed to incorporate opportunities for improving the efficiency of the work process while meeting the requirements of the PWS. The in-house bid is called the most efficient organization (MEO).

After all bids are submitted, contractor costs are formally compared with the MEO costs.[11] The contract cost includes the contract price (or bid) plus estimates of government contract monitoring and administrative expenses, and one-time transition costs. Contract costs also include the tax benefit that accrues to the government from having the service performed by a for-profit entity if the contractor is a for-profit organization. The MEO costs include estimates of the costs of operating the MEO and one-time transition costs. Starting in 1996, the MEO costs also have included a general and administrative

---

if they can perform the functions well). See Robbert, Gates, and Elliott (1997) for a discussion of these competing interests.

[9]Reasons are discussed in OMB Circular No. A-76—Revised Supplemental Handbook (March 1996), pp. 3–4.

[10]The PWS is sometimes referred to as the Statement of Work (SOW).

[11]The details of this process are described in OMB Circular No. A-76—Revised Supplemental Handbook (March 1996).

overhead charge equal to 12 percent of direct personnel costs.[12] The government first compares all external bids, and then compares the best of those to the MEO bid. Generally speaking, if the best contract bid is more than 10 percent below the MEO cost, the function will be contracted out.[13] Otherwise, the in-house organization wins the competition and must implement changes represented in the MEO.

A-76 as a DoD Cost Saving Strategy

DoD believes that A-76 competitions can generate substantial cost savings. The 1995 Commission on Roles and Missions of the Armed Forces gave special emphasis to expanded outsourcing of support services, advocating aggressive pursuit of this strategy. DoD plans to compete over 200,000 positions between FY 1997 and FY 2005 and expects savings of approximately $9 billion from those competitions, which are being programmed into service budgets.[14] These broad savings projections are based on an assumption that DoD will save between 20 and 30 percent on each billet competed.[15]

Excitement about the A-76 cost comparison process as a means of generating cost savings has been propelled by analyses conducted by the Center for Naval Analyses (CNA). Examining a set of completed DoD A-76 competitions, CNA has estimated that such competitions generated savings of approximately 30 percent per year (on average) for the government over the contract term: 38 percent for activities that are outsourced and 20 percent for activities that remain in house.[16]

In spite of past outsourcing efforts, there are still between 260,000 and 360,000 military and civilian positions eligible for an A-76 com-

---

[12]Prior to this, installations had complete flexibility in determining the estimated level of those overhead costs, and in most cases estimated them at zero.

[13]This 10 percent margin is designed to ensure that the government does not outsource a function in order to achieve marginal savings.

[14]See GAO/NSIAD-99-46.

[15]See GAO/NSIAD-99-66.

[16]See Tighe et al., 1996.

petition. For this reason, the notion of saving 20 to 30 percent on each billet is compelling.[17]

Limitations on Possible Cost Savings from A-76

There are, however, reasons to believe that the current expectations of potential savings from the A-76 process are overly optimistic[18] with regard to the process of conducting these competitions as well as the savings that will be generated from those that are completed.

The savings estimates generated by analysis of historical data have not been properly adjusted to account for practical aspects of implementation. In particular, savings are attributed to each billet slated for competition. However, historically, more than 40 percent of initiated competitions have been cancelled before completion (see Robbert, Gates, and Elliott (1997), Keating (1997)).[19] We have no data on the savings generated by cancelled competitions, but it is likely that those savings are low. When a competition is cancelled, the activity normally remains in house, and the in-house management is under no obligation to implement the MEO or otherwise improve efficiency. Moreover, Keating (1997) finds that competitions involving a large number of civilian billets are also the most frequently cancelled and subject to the longest delays.

---

[17]Robbert, Gates, and Elliott (1997) report that DoD-wide, 636,846 positions (302,956 of them military) categorized as commercial activities remained in-house at the end of FY 1994. For 268,044 (72,540 military) of these positions, there was no national defense reason for in-house performance. More recently, the Office of the Secretary of Defense for Acquisition and Technology (Installations) compiled service and agency responses to a call for reevaluation of commercial activities (Defense Reform Initiative Directive #20). Responding to this directive, OSD, the services, and agencies identified as of FY 1998, 618,506 military and civilian positions in commercial activities that are exempt from competitive sourcing for various reasons, and 283,594 that are not. Subsequent reevaluations by some components have raised the pool that is subject to competition to about 358,000. These numbers reflect interpretation on the part of the services in terms of which activities are classified as "commercial activities" and which commercial activities are exempt from the A-76 process for national defense reasons (Moore et al., 1997).

[18]See GAO/NSIAD-99-46 for a detailed discussion of these concerns.

[19]In defending the savings estimates, many have argued that the cancellation rate will decline because of increased high-level support for the A-76 process. We do not mean to suggest that the cancellation rate will remain at historically high levels. At the same time, there are many reasons for cancellation, and it is unlikely that the rate will fall to zero.

According to Tighe et al. (1996), these large competitions are precisely the types that have generated the largest percentage savings. Therefore, even if completed competitions yield savings on the order of 30 percent, the expected savings generated by each initiated competition are far less.

The number of positions scheduled for competition between FY 1997 and FY 2003 is more than twice the number competed by DoD between FY 1978 and FY 1996. Serious questions have been raised as to whether the DoD components can in fact identify the expected number of positions for competition in the first place, and whether the competitions can be completed in the anticipated time frame.

There are also concerns that the savings estimates for completed competitions fail to capture some important costs, particularly initial investment costs to conduct the competition and implement the contract or MEO (e.g., separation payments, hiring costs).

In spite of concerns over DoD's ability to achieve planned savings through the A-76 process, these savings have been programmed into DoD component budgets. OSD officials reported that "if the savings do not occur as quickly as planned, the components will have to absorb the shortfalls in their operations and maintenance accounts or shift money back from planned modernization."[20]

OBJECTIVES AND APPROACH

The purpose of this analysis is to develop a better understanding of the sources of efficiency improvement generated through the A-76 process, how those improvements are achieved, and whether they could be achieved outside of an A-76 competition. We focused our analysis on the use of personnel before and after A-76 competitions. At least half of DoD's overall infrastructure costs are personnel costs. Because A-76 competitions involve service activities, more than half of the costs of these activities probably are labor costs. Moreover, our sponsor for this research, the Deputy Assistant Secretary of Defense for Civilian Personnel Policy, has a special interest in the costs

_____

[20]See GAO/NSIAD-99-46, p.7.

and efficiencies of in-house workforces relative to external alternatives.

Our investigation explored four general questions:

- How big are the projected personnel cost savings?
- How are the projected personnel cost savings achieved?
- Are those savings real and enduring?
- Could the personnel cost savings be achieved outside of the A-76 process?

In order to examine these and other questions, we conducted a series of detailed case studies of recently completed and implemented A-76 competitions. The case studies involved detailed document reviews of the PWS, MEO, and, for outsourced activities, the contract file. We also gathered as much information as possible on current personnel. In addition, we conducted a series of semistructured interviews with various participants in all stages of the A-76 process and the contract or MEO implementation.

SCOPE

The results presented in this report are based on six case studies at four installations in three services (Army, Navy, and Air Force), and should be interpreted with appropriate caution. The number of candidate sites was limited because there was little A-76 activity in the early to mid-1990s. The installations we visited were among the select few that had actually completed A-76 competitions, and in many cases were breaking new ground—either in their service or in their command. These installations probably faced certain advantages and disadvantages that would not exist for installations conducting studies today; specifically, they likely had more resources available to complete the study but less experience with the process. It is also possible that some of the issues raised in these case studies are specific to the downsizing environment in which DoD currently finds itself.

This report refers in several places to policies and procedures promulgated by OMB or the Office of the Secretary of Defense (OSD).

While we have made every effort to capture the latest policies and procedures, changes are continually occurring, prompted by ongoing high-level executive and congressional interest in competitive sourcing. Readers should consult primary sources to obtain the most current policies and procedural guidance.

ORGANIZATION OF THE REPORT

In Chapter Two, we present our methodology, describing our initial hypotheses, the sites we visited, our information-gathering process, and the analytical approach. In Chapter Three, we present the main results related to the four basic research questions. We also discuss other issues that arose during our site visits. Chapter Four presents recommendations and conclusions. Appendix A includes our interview protocols; Appendix B summarizes the source of cost savings from each case study; Appendix C analyzes the contractor-government wage differences; and Appendix D discusses some of our concerns with the savings calculations in A-76 studies.

Chapter Two

METHODOLOGY

We examined the implementation of six completed A-76 cost comparison competitions to address the four questions listed in the first chapter. Our primary focus was on the use of personnel before and after the competition.

SITE SELECTION

We conducted case studies of six functions at four installations. To select the case studies for our analysis, we asked the A-76 representatives in the Army, Navy, Air Force, and Marine Corps to provide us with lists of installations that had completed and implemented an A-76 competition in the past ten years.

We identified candidate sites for our case studies in early 1998. In selecting the activities to be included in our study, we used several criteria.

- We targeted competitions that had been completed relatively recently, and for which the MEO or contract had been in place for at least one year. Recently completed competitions would ensure that most of the key participants in the cost comparison would still be at the installation. On the other hand, it was important that some time had elapsed after the implementation of the MEO or PWS so that we could evaluate the implementation, particularly changes in the use of personnel. Because there was a moratorium on the implementation of A-76 study results in the mid-1990s and a dramatic slowdown in the conduct of studies

was submitted by a contractor who proposed to perform all the functions, but this bid was 17 percent higher than the in-house bid.

BOS #2. This BOS solicitation included civil engineering, logistics, and transportation activities. The best contractor bid ended up being 15 percent less than the in-house bid, and therefore won the competition even after accounting for the 10 percent conversion differential.

Missile Maintenance (MM). This competition involved missile maintenance services being performed by one command for another as part of an interservice support agreement. The functions subject to competition were for routine missile repair and maintenance, including direct support and general support maintenance (DS/GS). Major repairs and overhauls, such as reparable exchange (RX) maintenance and depot level maintenance, were not included in the competition. The contract bid process for this function was an 8(a) competition, which means that it was directed by the Small Business Administration (SBA). The SBA identified a contractor believed to be capable of doing the work and asked it (and only it) to submit a bid. The contractor lost the competition by only 1 percent of MEO costs, after accounting for both the 10 percent conversion differential and the 12 percent overhead cost charge added to the in-house bid.

Aircraft Maintenance (AM) #1. This is the oldest cost-comparison competition included in our analysis, and the one involving the most positions. The original competition for this aircraft maintenance function was completed in 1989. Fortunately, all of the key players were still at the installation when we conducted this case study. The MEO cost was about 9 percent higher than the contractor cost, but the MEO won because of the 10 percent conversion differential.

AM #2. This cost-comparison competition involved the consolidation over time of activities conducted at different installations to a single site. This consolidation made it difficult to develop estimates of savings for this function, particularly in terms of the number of workers involved. The contractor won this competition by a tiny margin after accounting for the 10 percent conversion differential and the 12 percent overhead cost inflation factor applied to the in-house estimate.

Telecommunications Maintenance and Operation (TEL). This cost comparison decision was initially in favor of the MEO, but the decision was reversed on appeal by the contractor. The cost comparison inappropriately included some material costs in the contractor bid that were not present in the in-house bid. The function involves maintaining, operating, and monitoring specialized telecommunication equipment. The work requires many employees to have top-secret security clearances. After the completion of this competition, the service headquarters decided to close this facility, concluding that the activities could be eliminated or be performed elsewhere. The service already has eliminated several contract line items (CLINs) from the contract and is in the process of terminating the contract.

CASE STUDY STRUCTURE

Each case study involved document reviews and a wide range of interviews. At each site we requested the following documents:

- Contract solicitation, including the PWS

- Management study, including a description of the MEO

- Cost comparison study and/or the Commercial Activities Management Information Study (CAMIS) record

- Contract file, including any contract modifications (contractor wins only).

In addition, we requested information about the current workforce, such as authorizations, employment rosters, and other details. The nature of this information varied: Some installations kept detailed records of current employment, others did not. Generally, the information on contractor employees was much more limited than information on civil service workers.

We also conducted interviews at each installation with:

- Senior-level and/or intermediate-level commanders or staff managers responsible for the outsourced activity or MEO

- Government managers directly responsible for oversight of the outsourced activity or MEO

- Manpower office representatives
- Government contracting office representatives
- Civilian personnel office representatives
- Civil service employee union representatives
- Contractors' local managers (for contractor wins only).

In nearly every case, interviewees had had some involvement with the cost-comparison competition. In addition, at several installations we talked with current workers. Table A.1 in Appendix A summarizes the interviews we conducted at each installation, their purpose, and their duration.

The interviews were semistructured and followed a fixed interview protocol. The protocol is also in Appendix A.

HYPOTHESES

We began our investigation with four general questions related to the human resource efficiencies observed in competitively sourced activities.

Question 1: How big are the projected personnel cost savings?

As discussed earlier, analyses of historical A-76 data contained in previous studies by CNA reveal that completed A-76 competitions were projected to reduce baseline costs, on average, by 30 percent. A recent GAO study finds substantial expected savings on more recent competitions as well. Whereas previous studies look at total cost savings using CAMIS data, we attempt to isolate the personnel cost savings. Because personnel costs are a large fraction of the total costs for a service function, we do not expect our results to differ substantially from those of CNA or GAO. However, to the extent that cost savings stem disproportionately from personnel costs (as opposed to reductions in other costs), we would expect our estimates of personnel savings as a percentage of baseline personnel costs to be higher than the total cost savings as a percentage of total costs.

Question 2: How are the projected personnel cost savings achieved?

We anticipated that A-76 competitions would generate personnel cost savings in four generic ways. Organizations would use fewer people, downgrade existing positions, pay lower wages and benefits, or substitute capital for labor.[3]

Using Fewer People

Personnel reductions are an obvious and measurable way to reduce costs. Such reductions can be achieved in several ways: civilianization, multiskilling, organizational restructuring, increased work intensity, increased labor availability, and reduced work scope.

- *Civilianization.* Civilianization is the process of replacing military workers with civilian workers.[4] In the DoD, both military and civil service workers staff many commercial activities. An underlying assumption of the A-76 process is that cost savings can be achieved by substituting civilian for military labor.[5]

Civilianization can generate savings in two important ways: First, it might be possible to replace the current military workforce with fewer civilian workers; second, an individual military workyear may be more expensive than an individual civilian workyear. Conventional wisdom argues that military workers provide less workyear availability to the function in question because of training, deployment, and daily obligations such as physical training. Moreover, civilians are generally required to have the skills to do the job in order to be hired and tend to stay on the job for a long time. Military personnel on the other hand, often do not have the required skills when they assume a position. In addition, turnover is higher because military personnel must be rotated into and out of duties in

---

[3]Similar sources of productivity improvement in A-76 competitions were reported by Handy and O'Conner (1984).

[4]Civilianization may occur for reasons unrelated to cost (e.g., if military personnel are required for other duties). For the purposes of this report, we consider civilianization only from the cost-saving perspective.

[5]There is nothing that explicitly prohibits the MEO from including military workyears. However, we are not aware (either through case studies or data) of any MEO that included military personnel.

overseas areas, at sea, and in special functions such as recruiting or training. The need to continuously train new workers reduces an organization's efficiency.[6]

Any evaluation of the relative costs of individual military members versus individual civilian workers rests on a large number of assumptions about how each workforce is managed and what happens to the overall structure of the workforce when civilianization occurs at a local level.[7] Another crucial issue is whether the military positions eliminated through an A-76 competition are actually removed from the DoD workforce or are just used elsewhere. If the authorizations are not removed, DoD does not directly reap the savings from "eliminating" the military position. However, DoD may benefit indirectly from the ability to deploy the military personnel in areas where they can be more productive or in positions that were unfilled.

To the extent that civilianization is indeed an important source of savings, it will be more significant the greater the proportion of military personnel in the baseline workforce. Civilianization is available to both the in-house organization and the contractor. Thus, we have no reason to believe that the contractor would be more or less able to take advantage of the opportunities provided by civilianization.

- *Organizational restructuring.* Organizational restructuring can generate personnel savings by such methods as reducing the layers of management, streamlining work processes, and combining divisions and the required oversight. We anticipated organizational restructuring to be an important source of personnel savings, although we did not know which specific types would be most important. Organizational restructuring opportunities should be available to both the contractor and the in-house organization, and we have no reason to believe that one party has an inherent advantage. A contractor might be able to apply lessons learned from other contracts. Conversely, an in-house organization might experience inertia or a general reluctance to change. Alternatively, a contractor who does not

---

[6]On the other hand, many commanders and supervisors prefer military to civilian labor because military members can work overtime at no additional direct cost.

[7]Gates and Robbert (1998) discuss some of the issues involved in such a comparison.

understand the organizational structure and the work process as well as the in-house organization might be at a disadvantage.

- *Multiskilling.* Multiskilling can reduce the number of required workers by allowing one person to perform roles traditionally associated with two or more occupations. If each role requires less than a full-time worker, permitting one worker to perform them could save a fraction of a work-year. In so doing, multiskilling might also increase the work intensity of the workers who remain. Civil service rules and regulations do not prohibit the use of multiskilling within the government. However, because position descriptions for multiskilled jobs are not standard and because position descriptions are required for each job, government managers interested in using multiskilling may have to go through the process of getting a new job description approved and securing union support. Therefore, we hypothesize that contractors will be better able to take advantage of multiskilling. Government managers will be less likely to identify opportunities for multiskilling and less willing to go through the effort required to establish multiskilled positions.

- *Reduced work scope.* A service provider also might be able to reduce the number of workers relative to the baseline workforce if the scope of work is reduced. Reduced work scope is often associated with a reduction in quality or requirements. Alternatively, work scope might be altered because of changes in mission that are concurrent with the A-76 competition. Ultimately, the work requirements are determined by the PWS, not by the contract bid or MEO. The PWS might intentionally or unintentionally reduce the scope of work relative to the baseline level by eliminating certain activities, reducing quality standards, or eliminating certain work requirements.[8] If the PWS intentionally reduces the scope of work, then both the contractor and the in-house provider should be able to perform the work with fewer people. If the PWS unintentionally reduces the scope of work by omitting a function that is in fact required, it is likely that the contract will

---

[8]The reduction of work scope in the PWS is discussed by Robbert, Gates, and Elliott (1997), pp. 48–50. The authors report that there can be a tension between command headquarters, which is more inclined to reduce work scope in order to reduce costs, and installation commanders, who prefer an expanded work scope.

be modified to add that function or the MEO will be asked to perform the activity. As a result, unintentional reductions in the scope of work can result in contract cost escalation and possibly escalation in the cost of the MEO.

- *Improving work intensity or labor availability.* Fewer workers would be required if work intensity could be improved. Multi-skilling is one direct way to increase work intensity—if workers have more job responsibilities, they will tend to be busier and have less down time. Another way to increase work intensity is to improve worker motivation. Contractors sometimes argue that government employees are lazy and unmotivated because they know that firing them is difficult. Contractor employees may be motivated to do a good job because they know that they can be fired without the extensive due-process procedures that apply to civil service workers. Additionally, contractors have more flexibility to use contingent rewards such as bonuses, gain-sharing, and profit-sharing. Finally, as suggested by CNA (1996), contractors might have more flexibility to use part-time or temporary workers. This ability could increase work intensity because workers can be called in on an as-needed basis. Contractors might have improved labor availability if they offer less time off (sick time and vacation).

Downgrading Existing Positions

Another mechanism for reducing costs is to downgrade existing positions. This downgrade is accomplished either by reducing the required grade and skill level in existing positions or by changing the grade structure of the workforce (e.g., using more helpers and fewer journeymen). Position descriptions for government employees are supposed to be reviewed periodically to ensure that the tasks performed warrant the assigned grade levels; however, assigned grade levels might be too high (or too low) because the tasks actually performed by the individual have changed over time. An A-76 competition provides an opportunity for both the in-house organization and the contractor to evaluate the required skills in view of the work that needs to be performed. Although both are able to downgrade positions, we expect it to be easier for the contractor because the contractor need not be as concerned with the incumbent currently holding a particular position. In addition, the Department of Labor

(DoL) job classification rules for service contractors are often less precise than Office of Personnel Management (OPM) classification standards, which apply to civil service workers. For example, whereas the DoL classification rules have only one type of aircraft mechanic, the OPM classification standards have a separate category (and two levels) for an aircraft engine repairer.

Paying Lower Wages and Benefits

Lower wages should be a source of savings only relative to the baseline organization when the contractor wins the study. The government has no opportunity to pay lower wages without downgrading positions because the grade level of the position, the step of the employee, and the location where the work takes place determine wages. The contractor could reduce personnel costs by paying a particular type of worker a wage that is lower than the government wage. However, the Service Contract Act (SCA) places a floor on the wages and benefits that contractors can pay employees.[9] These restrictions vary with the position in question, so that there is one wage and benefit floor for a journeyman aircraft mechanic and another (lower) floor for a lower-skilled aircraft mechanic helper.[10] Although no fixed relationship exists between government wages and benefits and contractor mandated minimums, contractor wages and benefits are generally assumed to be lower than government wages and benefits. Therefore, we expected lower employment costs to be a source of savings in competitions won by the contractor.

Capital-Labor Substitution

We expected there to be opportunities for contractors to take advantage of capital-labor substitution in order to reduce personnel costs.

---

[9]The Service Contract Act (41 USC 351 et seq.) requires private contractors to pay wages and provide fringe benefits equal to or greater than the larger of (1) prevailing wage rates (as determined by a DoL survey) for a particular job in a particular area, or (2) wage rates determined in accordance with a collective bargaining agreement. If a collective bargaining agreement is reached during the life of a contract, the direct costs associated with that agreement are generally passed on to the government if the DoL deems the agreement reasonable.

[10]Because these wage floors are determined by surveys of prevailing wages in the local area, they can vary geographically.

Question 3: Are the personnel cost savings real and enduring?

Numerous issues relate to cost savings estimates. How valid are the available data on expected savings? To what degree will expected savings be realized in the long run? Although we did not expect to reach definitive conclusions about these issues in the course of this study, we hoped to learn a bit more about the validity of these concerns.

Projections of savings from future A-76 competitions are generated by calculating the historical average of the expected cost savings as recorded in the CAMIS database and applying that savings rate to estimates of future competitions. Thus, the projections assume that current opportunities for cost savings are similar to those that existed in the past.

The CAMIS savings estimates reflect cost savings from the implementation of the MEO or the contract. These estimates are developed by comparing a baseline cost with the estimated cost of the winning bid. These cost estimates include personnel costs (both direct and indirect). Other costs common to the MEO and contractor operations, such as utilities, facilities, and maintenance, are normally excluded from the cost comparison.

GAO (1990) has expressed concern with the quality of these savings estimates. Among other things, the estimates often fail to account for the costs of retained grade and pay, future wage increases mandated by the OPM or the SCA, or the expected value of contractor bonus payments or award fees. Such costs can persist for many years. Moreover, GAO (1999) has found no DoD-wide guidance as to a method for calculating baseline costs. With the exception of the Air Force, there is no service-wide guidance on this topic either. Ultimately, little consensus exists as to what these numbers mean and whether they can be compared between sites.

Another concern is that CAMIS often only estimates the initial cost savings to be generated by an A-76 competition. Little is known about whether these cost savings are realized or persist over time because, in our experience, components have seldom complied with CAMIS requirements to reflect actual costs during the performance period. New guidance on this subject (Yim, 1999) has been issued.

A GAO (1991) review of an Army contract at Ft. Sill suggests that contract costs can exceed not only the initial bid but also the bid of the losing in-house organization. Comparing the actual contract costs with estimates of what it would have cost the Army to perform the function in-house, the GAO concluded that in-house performance would have been substantially less costly. It attributed the higher contractor costs to contractor employee pay increasing at a faster rate than that of federal employees and to higher-than-expected contract administration costs.

Contract costs also can escalate if the contractor requests additional payment for work that was not specifically stipulated by the contract. Government workers often complain that contract costs escalate because contractors underbid. Contractors often claim that contract costs increase because the initial PWS was inadequate (see Robbert, Gates, and Elliott, 1997). While such cost escalation is easily identified because it is recorded in the contract file, it would not be reflected in the CAMIS records upon which the cost savings estimates are based.

When the PWS reduces the scope of work relative to the baseline organization, there is a particular danger that the estimated cost savings will not be achieved or sustained. The scope could be increased again after implementation when the managers realize the implications of the reduced scope. This cycle could lead to an increase in the cost of both the MEO and the contract. Alternatively, the work might be absorbed by other functions. In this case, the cost increases would be hidden in the budgets of that function and the cost savings for the competition would be overestimated.

Our previous research suggests that a lack of follow-up also can affect the estimates of the cost of MEO performance (Robbert, Gates, and Elliott, 1997). For example, grade creep, wage increases, or inflation in the number of in-house workers may increase the costs of the MEO.

Question 4: Could the savings be achieved outside the A-76 process?

There are widespread concerns that DoD will be unable to complete the targeted number of competitions in the required time frame.

Since an analysis of historical data (see Tighe et al., 1996) suggests that cost savings are generated through competition both for MEO and contractor wins, we considered whether a review of past competitions could identify strategies to improve workforce efficiency that could occur without an A-76 competition.

DoD has a long history of conducting A-76 competitions, and it is useful to understand the source of the efficiency improvements generated through the previous competitions in order to determine whether lessons exist that could be applied to activities within DoD that are not subject to competition for one reason or another. Few have conducted follow-up studies to understand the source of those savings generated by competitive sourcing or to apply those lessons more broadly. Among the few examples of the latter are RAND studies from the 1970s that attempted to draw lessons learned by comparing outsourced activities at Vance Air Force Base, OK, with similar activities at Reese Air Force Base, TX (Paulson and Zimmer, 1975; Shishko, Paulson, and Perry, 1977). This research concluded that DoD could save money by applying several contractor management principles observed at Vance at other installations. A Logistics Management Institute study has also highlighted productivity improvements motivated by competition (Handy and O'Conner, 1984). Interestingly, the notion of deriving lessons learned and applying them in activities not subject to competitive sourcing has not been revived in the current environment.

As discussed above, some activities will never be subject to the A-76 process, either because they are inherently governmental or because, although commercial, they are important to national defense and cannot be outsourced. Even for activities slated for a cost comparison, the study may not be initiated in the near term, and the government could save money by initiating some of these changes in activities that are not immediately subject to competition.[11]

_____

[11]A-76 competitions take, on average, approximately two years to complete. Provisions within the FY 1991 and all subsequent Defense Appropriations Acts have required that competitions not completed within two years (four years for a multifunction study) to be cancelled. Although this requirement might provide an incentive for speeding up the competitions, it may also increase the cancellation rate. Service representatives counter that they have some measure of control over the cancellation rate, and that if top level management is behind the A-76 process, more competitions will be completed. While it is impossible to quibble with this logic, it is also true that

Through interviews we tried to identify whether there was something special about the A-76 process that generates savings that could not be achieved without such competition and to discern ways in which cost savings could be achieved in functions that are not under study.

ANALYSIS AND SOURCES OF INFORMATION

The analysis relies on two primary sources of data: A-76 competition documents and interviews. We culled the documents for data and factual descriptions. In most cases, we obtained the CAMIS record and the management study documents before our site visit. We gathered other documents during site visits. The interviews provided a context for the data as well as information that was not available in the documents.

Magnitude of Personnel Cost Savings

As a first step in our analysis, we constructed a measure of the expected initial personnel cost savings from the A-76 studies.[12] Information on the magnitude of the cost savings comes largely from the document review. The documents contain detailed information about the baseline number of personnel and the estimated cost of the baseline workforce, position by position. In the case of MEO wins, the documents contain similarly detailed information about the proposed in-house workforce. On the basis of this information, we were able to construct rough estimates of the magnitude of the personnel-related savings.

Developing a measure of personnel cost savings that we could use across all competitions, whether won by the contractor or the MEO, was a major challenge. To the extent possible, we have isolated the personnel costs and related overhead costs and consider those only when calculating the savings. Thus, our savings estimates reflect personnel cost savings achieved through the A-76 process as a per-

---

management cannot control all the factors contributing to cancellation. In particular, if local managers are opposed, they may be able to sabotage the process.

[12]These estimates are similar to the estimates of expected initial cost savings found in CAMIS and in other analyses. Later, we consider whether these saving were achieved and whether they endure over time.

centage of baseline personnel costs. The personnel cost savings percentage estimates reflect the cost reduction achieved in the first year of the contract or MEO implementation. We base the calculations on current (at the time of the A-76 competition) dollars.

Our first step in calculating the personnel cost savings percentage was to develop an estimate of the annual cost of personnel performing the function before the A-76 study. We refer to this as the baseline cost. *Baseline personnel* cost estimates were calculated using information contained in the cost study documents and include direct personnel costs such as wages, benefits, and other pay, as well as indirect personnel costs such as overhead associated with the baseline organization.

Alternatively, we could have focused on the *total* costs of performing a function when calculating the percentage savings. We did not do so for two reasons. First, our research sponsor has a specific interest in personnel-related phenomena. Second, nonpersonnel costs (material and equipment costs and the costs of reimbursables) are not treated in a consistent way in these cost comparison studies. Sometimes the government provides the materials and equipment and their cost are omitted from the competition; sometimes, the government provides them but their costs are included. In other studies, the contractor is required to provide the materials. On occasion the arrangement is something in-between. The lack of standard practice on this issue can be the source of confusion, even among those intimately involved in the process. For example, in the TEL competition, the initial decision was for the MEO. The contractor won on appeal, because the contract bid was required to include materials costs that were left out of the in-house bid.

In most cases, management study documents contained cost information. However, the TEL competition contained staffing but not personnel cost information. Therefore, we had to estimate the personnel cost using detailed information on the baseline organization staffing along with cost estimates for military and civil service personnel contained in Gates and Robbert (1998).[13]

---

[13]The estimates were adjusted based on differences between the predicted and actual MEO costs.

We did not simply use the cost savings estimates as reported by the installations. In several cases, we modified those estimates based on other information in the documents. Specifically, we excluded *authorized* positions that were not filled and were scheduled for elimination.

Our baseline personnel cost estimates include general and administrative overhead charges (as indirect costs) if such charges were applied to MEO personnel costs during the competition. Before 1996, installations had discretion as far as what overhead rate to apply and most included no indirect overhead costs in the MEO bid. In 1996, the rules changed and installations were required to add an overhead charge of 12 percent of MEO personnel costs to the total MEO bid.[14] If the in-house bid has an overhead personnel charge, then the same percentage rate was applied to the baseline personnel costs to calculate total baseline personnel costs.[15] The 12 percent rate was applied in the TEL and MM calculations.[16]

Once we estimated the baseline personnel costs, we estimated the expected annual personnel costs for the first year of the MEO or contract performance as reflected in the MEO or contract bid. For MEO wins, MEO expected personnel costs estimates were readily available from the cost-comparison study documents. These costs included the direct personnel costs plus the personnel overhead charge, if applicable, plus any transition costs[17] (amortized over the entire performance period). In contractor wins, we calculated total contractor personnel cost by taking the contract price, subtracting any direct materials cost, adding any contract monitoring and one-time transition costs (amortized over the life of the contract), and

---

[14]See GAO/NSIAD-98-62.

[15]The inclusion of the 12 percent overhead charge has no impact on the estimate of cost savings as a percentage of baseline personnel costs when the in-house bid wins because it is applied to both the baseline personnel cost estimate and the in-house bid. In cases where the contract bid wins, the application of the 12 percent overhead charge to the baseline personnel cost will inflate the cost savings estimates.

[16]Thus, the TEL competition is the only one for which the application of the 12 percent overhead charge to baseline personnel costs will influence the initial savings estimates. We report the savings estimate excluding these overhead charges in a footnote.

[17]These transition costs refer to the costs associated with implementing the MEO.

subtracting the tax advantage that accrues to the government.[18] This information is available from A-76 competition documents.[19] The total contractor personnel cost thus provides a good estimate of the effective cost of contractor personnel to the government after considering the contractor's profit, monitoring costs, and the tax advantage.

With personnel cost estimates for the organization before and after the A-76 study in hand, our final step was to calculate a cost savings percentage. To do this, we took the baseline personnel costs, subtracted the MEO or contractor personnel costs, and then divided the difference by the baseline personnel costs.

We could not follow this estimation procedure when analyzing the savings generated by the AM #2 competition. This function involved the consolidation of activities performed at several installations by a mix of contract and government employees. The management study did not include detailed information on the broad "baseline organization," just on the baseline organization of the installation that was submitting the MEO bid. As a result, we had to rely on savings estimates found in the CAMIS record. To calculate percentage savings, we divided the savings estimate by the estimate of baseline costs as reported in CAMIS. The PWS focused on the provision of labor service. The government provided all supplies and equipment. Therefore, the savings estimates reflected in CAMIS should closely mirror personnel cost savings.

In addition to estimates of personnel cost savings, we also calculated the percentage savings in the number of personnel billets. This calculation followed the same procedures described above, using the number of personnel billets in place of personnel cost estimates.

---

[18]Contract performance provides the contractor with income that is subject to federal income tax. Unless the contractor is a tax-exempt organization, an estimate of these taxes is deducted from the net cost to the government.

[19]The contract cost does not include the 10 percent differential or "disadvantage" that the contract bid must overcome to win the competition against the MEO.

Sources of Savings

The information on the sources of savings stems from a combination of document review and interviews. For in-house wins, the savings sources were reasonably easy to identify from the documents. For example, we observed when military positions were civilianized or eliminated, or when positions were downgraded. These management study documents also described major organizational restructuring efforts. Where possible, we also analyzed the difference between the DoL wage rates (minimum contractor wages mandated by the Service Contract Act) and the civil service wages for that region.

The management study documents often present the MEO and baseline organization personnel side by side with notations as to the positions that have been modified or deleted from the organization. For contractor wins, we had to rely more heavily on interview data because the documents reviewed did not contain information on personnel use.

Persistence of Savings

We relied on document review and interviews to evaluate the persistence of the personnel cost savings. For contractor wins, we examined all contract modifications, highlighting those that led to an increase or decrease in contract costs. In each of the competitions examined, the contractors and the MEO submitted bids for five performance periods, where a performance period is equal to one year. The bids for each performance period incorporate expectations about inflation, changes in workload, and other factors that might affect the cost over time. Thus we were able to compare the bid for a particular contract performance period with the actual cost of the contract for that period. In addition, we examined the explanation for those changes found in the contract modification.

For MEO wins, we were able to obtain information only on authorizations by position and grade level. Although this availability does allow for a reasonable comparison between the MEO bid[20] and the

---

[20]In each case, the MEO bid the same number of personnel for all five performance periods, so we compare that number of slots with the current personnel slots.

current in-house organization, we must point out that personnel authorizations do not fully reflect personnel costs. In particular, this approach did not allow us to evaluate the cost impact of retained pay, step increases, or staffing problems. For MEO wins, we thus examined the current authorization list and compared it with the number of authorizations bid in the MEO. We report explanations for those changes, which either were found in the CAMIS record updates or were discussed in the interviews.

Other Ways to Improve Government Efficiency

Information on whether it would be possible to achieve these types of efficiencies outside of the A-76 process was derived almost exclusively from interviews, and the results in this section should be viewed with appropriate caution.

Chapter Three

RESULTS

This chapter presents the results of our analysis. We begin by presenting estimates of personnel cost savings from each A-76 competition. We then summarize the sources of those savings on a case-by-case basis. Next, we discuss the differences between civil service and contractor wages. We conclude with information on the persistence of savings.

QUESTION 1: HOW BIG ARE THE PROJECTED PERSONNEL COST SAVINGS?

The expected personnel cost savings from the A-76 competitions were substantial for both in-house and contractor wins, ranging from 34 to 59 percent of baseline personnel costs.

Figure 3.1 summarizes the projected personnel cost savings as a percentage of the baseline cost for each function. The expected savings ranged from 41 to 59 percent for contractor wins, and from 34 to 59 percent for in-house wins.[1] They are generally much greater than the 20–30 percent overall savings estimates generated from historical data.

---

[1]If we exclude the 12 percent overhead charge from the baseline personnel cost estimate in the TEL competition, then the initial expected personnel cost savings are 34 percent rather than 59 percent. The difference is substantial and reflects the importance of assumptions about overhead personnel costs. It also calls for careful consideration of whether the 12 percent rate reflects real overhead costs, and hence real savings, in the event of outsourcing.

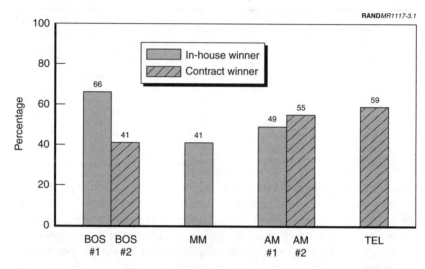

Figure 3.1 —Expected Post-Competition Costs as a Percentage of Baseline Costs

Figure 3.2 provides information on projected personnel reductions for the functions for which such information was available. Staffing information was not available for the BOS #2 and AM #2 contracts, so we could not calculate personnel billet savings for those functions.

Figure 3.2 reveals that expected personnel reductions stemming from the A-76 competition are substantial, ranging from 24 to 60 percent. The personnel reductions appear to track the overall cost reductions, suggesting that reduction in the number of billets is the chief component of personnel cost savings. However, we note that the percentage reductions in personnel may be more or less than the percentage reductions in cost. This range suggests possible differences in the way personnel costs are reduced.

Figure 3.3 presents projected personnel cost and slot savings information for each function included in the BOS #1 competition. Such detailed information was not available for the BOS #2 competition. This disaggregation suggests that savings can vary dramatically by function, even within a single installation. For example, the

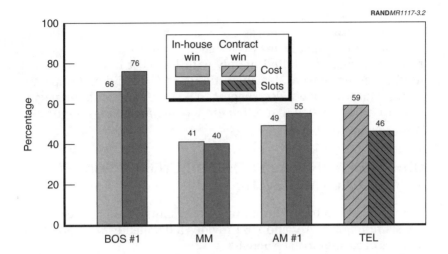

Figure 3.2 —Expected Post-Competition Personnel Costs and Slots as a
Percentage of Baseline

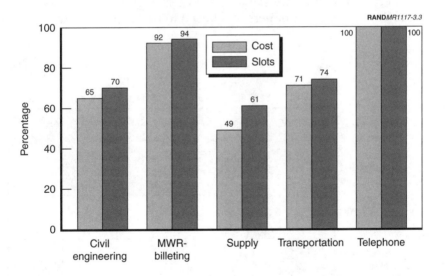

Figure 3.3—Expected Post-Competition Personnel Costs and Slots as a
Percentage of Baseline in the BOS #1 Study

telephone operator function is one that requires full-time, around-the-clock staffing. There was no room for personnel reduction in that function. Similarly, the MWR billeting function baseline organization was already staffed mainly with low-cost nonappropriated fund (NAF) employees, leaving little room for additional improvement. Our interviews also suggest that some functional managers were more aggressive than others in looking for savings opportunities.

QUESTION 2: HOW ARE THE PROJECTED PERSONNEL COST SAVINGS ACHIEVED?

Figure 3.4 summarizes the sources of personnel cost savings across the six functions. Appendix B provides a detailed exposition of the sources of savings in each activity.

As indicated in Figure 3.4, no significant difference appears in the source of cost savings between the contractor and the in-house wins. In every competition we examined, cost savings were generated by reducing the number of personnel used to perform the work. Most

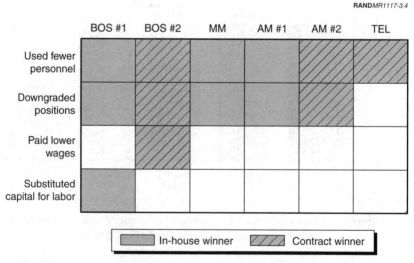

Figure 3.4—Summary of Sources of Projected Personnel Cost Savings

of the in-house and contractor winners also reduced costs by down-grading positions. Surprisingly, lower wages were a factor in the activities cost reduction for only one function. Finally, the substitution of capital for labor was a factor in generating cost savings for only one function (BOS #1), and then it was a minor one.

Using Fewer Workers

Clearly an important way to reduce the cost of an activity is to perform it with fewer workers. But how can an activity be accomplished with fewer workers? What changes allow for such an improvement in efficiency? In the previous chapter, we hypothesized that several strategies might enable an organization to perform work with fewer people: civilianization, multiskilling, organizational restructuring, reduced work scope, and increased work intensity or labor availability.

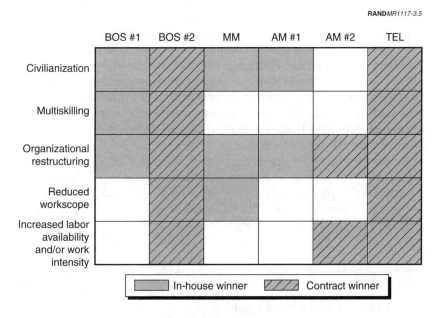

RAND*MR1117-3.5*

Figure 3.5—Summary of Strategies Used to Reduce the
Size of the Workforce

Figure 3.5 summarizes the approaches the in-house and contractor winners took to reduce the workforce.[2] With the exception of in creased labor availability, which was used only by contractors, the MEO seems to use the same labor-saving techniques as contractors to reduce the size of the workforce.

Civilianization

Civilianization played a significant role in workforce reduction. As suggested in Figure 2.1, each function except AM #2 used a significant number of military personnel in its baseline structure. In each case, the post-study workforce was completely civilian, either contractor or government civil service. Of course, the fact that military positions were civilianized does not directly imply that this transformation was the source of savings. The link between civilianization and cost savings required a more detailed analysis.

The major benefit of civilianization is the ability of the organization to perform the function with fewer workers. This benefit is often amplified through one or more other avenues, such as organizational restructuring or increased labor availability. If the MEO won, civilianization was accompanied by organizational restructuring in part because certain formal organizational changes are *required* when military personnel are eliminated from a function. For example, in BOS #1, the functional manager reported that squadrons were eliminated because the commander of a squadron must be a military person and all the military positions were being eliminated. Each function reported that eliminating requirements that come with a military workforce helped flatten their organizations or reduce the number of supervisors or managers. In the TEL competition, cutting military personnel eliminated several intermediate-level management positions. Civilianization also eliminated the training officer positions. In AM #1, civilianization substantially reduced the number of supervisory positions.

---

[2]Isolating one labor-saving strategy from another is often difficult. For example, civilianization allows for (or even demands) organizational restructuring. To the extent possible, we discuss the contribution of different strategies to the organization's ability to perform the work with fewer people.

Several functional managers noted that by improving labor availability civilianization reduced their need for workers. Perhaps the most extreme example of this was MM, where military positions were eliminated because the uniformed labor was completely unavailable to the function in question. In AM #1, the MEO included one civil service worker for every two military positions eliminated. Managers at each site reported that they lost a lot of time from their military personnel to detailing, physical training, and deployment; a civilian workforce is much more predictable. Indeed, several people involved in developing the MM MEO mentioned that the standard rule used in that command to estimate the number of civil service workers needed is .6 civilians for each military person.

Civilianization also can allow for other changes in the way work is organized. In AM #1, it allowed for the establishment of labor progression structures that included helpers and intermediate and journeyman laborers, rather than the journeyman-intensive structure that was inherent in the military workforce. In TEL, workers reported that when the function was being performed in-house, eight different military workers were detailed for some amount of time to clean the building. In addition, there was a contract for grounds maintenance. Now, the contractor has one person who does all the cleaning and grasscutting.

Finally, civilianization can save money independent of the number of slots saved if the military personnel are replaced by civilians. Opportunities for such savings were perhaps most evident in BOS #1, where we observed an instance where a wide range of military personnel (E-3 to E-6) was replaced by GS-4 civil service workers on the billeting desk.

Multiskilling

Multiskilling was another important source of savings in one MEO win and two contractor wins. Perhaps the clearest benefit from multiskilling came in TEL, where the contractor cross-trained workers and combined two independent job series, leading to a dramatic reduction in requirements. Multiskilling also was important in both BOS competitions, where generalized clerks and other workers could be used in several functional areas.

In the MM MEO win, multiskilling was not a source of savings per se because the job descriptions of the key civil service workers were already quite general—multiskilling was already being used.

Multiskilling was not a factor in the two AM competitions for two apparent reasons. First, the job descriptions for aircraft maintenance workers are fairly constrained by the PWS. Workers in a certain category are required to have specific training or experience within a certain time frame to qualify for a position. The contractor or MEO cannot simply disregard or modify these requirements. Secondly, in the case of AM #1, the sheer magnitude of the activity reduced the incidence of fractional manpower requirements and therefore reduced the potential gains from multiskilling and increased the relative gains to specialization.

We had anticipated that there would be formal or informal barriers to the use of multiskilling that would make it more difficult for the MEO to use this technique. However, we found none. Government managers are generally aware that they can use multiskilling and seem to use it when appropriate. The functional managers in the BOS #1 study reported that DoD or OPM has no regulations to prohibit it. They noted, however, a requirement to pay workers for the highest-graded regular and recurring activity they perform.[3] To use multiskilling cost-effectively, it is necessary to build a position description that ensures that the primary task of the individual is the more expensive one.

We observed employee resistance to multiskilling. In BOS #1, the union representatives with whom we spoke complained that the MEO was using more multiskilling, generally without offering workers a higher salary. He explained that because workers have more tasks to perform, the pace of work is more intense. The union representatives believe that this amounted to a "change in working conditions" and noted that the union had filed a grievance over this issue. The functional manager at MM also mentioned that after the MEO won, workers petitioned for grade increases because of multiskilling.

---

[3]See U.S. Office of Personnel Management, *FWS Job Grading System, Part I: Explanation of the FWS Job Grading System*, June 1997, p. 8; *FWS Job Grading for Supervisors*, Dec. 1997, p. 25; and *Introduction to the Position Classification Standards*, Dec. 1996, pp. 17–18.

The workers of the winning TEL function, although happy to have jobs with the contractor, complained about multiskilling. As discussed earlier, multiskilling required technicians to perform more mundane operator duties as well. Again, some dissatisfaction accompanied the increased work intensity. However, this dissatisfaction was tempered because the contractor could pay workers a wage premium for performing multiple skills, and workers indeed got a raise when they went to work for the contractor.

On the other hand, the government is restricted by law from paying a worker a multiskilling premium beyond the highest wage for the grade level associated with a regular and recurring task performed by that worker. The government has no flexibility to pay the worker more than the wage of that grade level, even if it is unusual for those skills to be acquired by one individual and if it benefits the government greatly to have one individual with both skills. This restriction is particularly important in cases where the grade level assigned to each task is the same and thus an employee in a multiskilled position receives the same wage as an employee in a regular position.[4]

Organizational Restructuring

Organizational restructuring can generate cost savings independent of civilianization. For example, in AM #2 the contractor modified processes that were already being performed by civil service employees so that the tasks could be done by fewer workers. In BOS #2, the contractor eliminated distinctions between certain functional areas. In so doing, the contractor was able to eliminate some mid-level managers. MM consolidated the repair functions to one location, thereby reducing delays and streamlining the work process. Moreover, the MM MEO added a production clerk position that was responsible for managing work orders. Again, this adjustment allowed for a more efficient allocation of workload across the mechanics.

----

[4]Our interviews with civilian personnel officers suggest that managers and classification specialists are extremely careful in creating multiskilled positions for group tasks at the same grade level to avoid paying a premium. However, the government can pay recruitment bonuses and retention allowances.

Reduced Work Scope

An A-76 competition can reduce the work scope of the activity under study either explicitly or implicitly. It is explicit if reduced work scope is written into the PWS. An A-76 competition provides an important opportunity for cost savings to be achieved through downscoping. Because costs are highly visible during an A-76 competition, customers are confronted—often for the first time—with the trade-off between the cost and quality of service. In developing the PWS, the customers can examine the trade-offs and choose a more reasonable level of service. This important source of cost savings would probably not be achieved without the A-76 competition.

Such a clearly and consciously reduced work scope was the source of savings in two competitions: MM and TEL. In both cases, determining the overall impact of the savings was difficult because the downscoped activities were transferred to other organizations. The costs of these other organizations are not included in the A-76 analyses, and therefore we have no measure of the costs this transfer imposes on those organizations.[5]

Implicit downscoping, in which the requirements contained in the PWS were unintentionally reduced, may have occurred in several other competitions, particularly AM #2, BOS #2, and BOS #1. Identifying implicit downscoping is difficult. Poor performance might be the result of implicit downscoping because the PWS established unacceptably low quality standards. Similarly, escalation in the contract price or MEO authorizations might result from implicit downscoping because the PWS underestimates the workload and the additional work must be written back into the contract. But not all poor per-

---

[5]The savings for the downscoped function may have been overestimated if the organization to which workloads were transferred needed to hire additional people to perform those functions. In the MM case, the function manager claimed that the customer organization did not have to hire any new people. In the TEL case, staff reported that the functions were simply absorbed by the existing staff. We were not able to verify these claims. Moreover, the worker who had been responsible for coordinating with Defense Information Services Agency (DISA) in the previous in-house organization reported that it was unrealistic to regionalize the function because many tasks involved in the function need to be performed on-site. The employee reports that although the function has been officially "regionalized," much of the work is still done at that installation and is simply being absorbed by other workers.

formance or expansion of workload is a reflection of implicit down-scoping. Thus, to identify implicit downscoping, we were forced to rely on the opinions of individuals involved in developing the MEO and in monitoring the contract.[6]

Civilianization of military positions involves another form of implicit downscoping. Units with military personnel must generally make those individuals available to support periodic deployments and must also invest in the human capital development (e.g., physical training and general military training) necessary to keep them ready for deployment. When functions are civilianized, total service deployment requirements are unaffected. The burden of supporting these requirements is transferred to other units.

Labor Availability/Increased Work Intensity

Contractors were able to perform work with fewer employees by improving labor availability and increasing work intensity. Contractors improve labor availability by offering less leave time or placing more restrictions on the time that they make available. In the TEL case, the contractor hired former government employees with many years of experience in the civil service. These workers receive ten days of leave per year with the contractor (as opposed to the 26 days they were receiving from the government) and they are paid for the days that they do not use within a fixed time frame.[7] The TEL contractor also noted that he has dramatically cut training-related absences by reducing the amount of training and encouraging on-site training through CD-ROM. The AM #2 contractor also noted that contractor workers have less leave and sick time. These policies increase labor availability because workers spend more time on the job.

The BOS #2 and AM #2 contractors also noted that their ability to hire and fire at will improved work intensity. This ability affects work intensity in two ways: it causes workers to work harder because they know they can be fired if they do not do a good job, and it allows contractors to have fewer workers on the payroll because they can

---

[6]See the summaries in Appendix B for more information on these issues.

[7]Contractor employees are entitled to more leave time as they accrue more seniority with a contractor. Workers are entitled to a minimum of ten days after one year of service, 15 days after ten years, and 20 days after 20 years.

adjust their workforces more quickly to changing needs. We cannot measure the impact these opportunities have on the contractor workforce, although all of the contractors reported that their man-hour availability factors are higher than the government's.

Downgrading Positions

Downgrading individual positions, or changing the grade structure of the workforce so as to lower the average grade level of employees, was an important source of savings in all of the studies that remained in-house. As discussed above, in AM #1, the MEO made more use of helper and intermediate level workers, and created progression structures so that workers could eventually achieve a journeyman skill level. In MM, the MEO revised the job descriptions to reflect more closely the work actually being performed, leading to a greater relative reduction in the number of WG-13 mechanics versus WG-12 mechanics.[8] While the BOS #1 study did not lead to an overall change in the grade structure, there were pockets of grade increases and pockets of grade decreases. In one area (Civil Engineering), many positions were in fact downgraded to WG-2 positions only to be upgraded later to WG-5 positions upon appeal to the civilian personnel office. This result suggests that there are checks in the system that allow the government to downgrade positions only if the original position descriptions were inflated or if the work could be reorganized.

Contractors also downgraded positions to reduce costs. The BOS #2 contractor put in place more low-level personnel such as clerks and helper workers. The AM #2 contractor used fewer foremen, thereby lowering the grade structure of the workforce. However, not all contractors downgraded positions. The TEL contractor, for example,

------

[8]Federal civil service jobs are often described by pay plan and grade level. The number refers to the grade level, and can range from 1 to 15. The letters refer to the pay plan. Four pay plans cover over 85 percent of the civil service workforce (and a vast majority of the positions examined in an A-76 study): General Schedule (GS), Wage Grade (WG), Wage Leader (WL), and Wage Supervisor (WS). The GS governs white collar positions whereas the WG/WL/WS schedules govern blue-collar positions. In total there are over 70 different pay plans, many of which apply to highly specialized groups of employees.

upgraded the workforce by hiring people for multiskilled positions at higher pay than they had received from the government.

Paying Lower Wages

To determine whether lower wages were an important source of cost savings, we compared the wage and benefit costs of the baseline workforce with the wages of the workforce reflected in the winning contractor or MEO bid. The details of those wage comparisons are described in Appendix C. Figure 3.4 indicates that lower wages were a source of cost savings for only one study, BOS #2.

Contractors sometimes pay their employees wages that are lower than government wages. Because the SCA restricts contractor wages and benefits for service employees, the actual employment cost of contractor employees can be higher or lower than the cost of federal employees in similar positions.

Several factors influence the magnitude and direction of the differential. Robbert, Gates, and Elliott (1997) discuss the wage determination issue and the distortions that can be introduced into the process. DoL wage surveys used to establish minimum contractor wages for specific jobs are based on simple averages in the local area. Federal Wage System (FWS)[9] wage rates for civil service employees are determined by regressing local average wages for various jobs on matching FWS grade levels. A wide variety of occupations might fall into a given grade level, and the market wages for those positions might vary dramatically.

Benefits can also differ between FWS jobs and DoL wage surveys. OMB sets forth benefits cost factors (a percentage rate applied to base pay) to be used when conducting a cost comparison study. The same cost factor is applied to both FWS and GS positions. These rates change from year to year. Two 1995 cost comparison studies we scrutinized used a rate of 29.55 percent of base pay. In contrast, DoL wage surveys for the corresponding area specified a fringe benefit rate for "health and welfare" of no less than a flat hourly rate

---

[9]The FWS governs the pay and benefits for hourly blue-collar workers in the federal government.

Table 3.1

Annual Leave Accrual Rates for Civil Service and Service Contractor Employees

Years of Service	Civil Service Leave Accrual (days per year)	Service Contractor Leave Accrual (minimum days per year)
Less than 1	13	0
1 to 3	13	10
3 to 5	19.5	10
5 to 15	19.5	15
more than 15	26	20

of $2.56, regardless of the wage rate. In addition, the contractor is responsible to pay the employer's portion of FICA and Medicare taxes. At this level, fringe benefits for "health and welfare" ranged from 18.1 percent of the $14.15 hourly wage of an aircraft mechanic to 34.3 percent of the $7.46 hourly wage of a material handling laborer.

As depicted in Table 3.1, federal civil service vacation days are generally more generous than minimums for workers subject to the SWA. The implicit cost of time off is not included in the wage comparison information. Federal civil servants have ten paid holidays per year, and this is also the SCA minimum number of holidays for the activities we studied.

Lower wages can lead to a decrease in overall personnel costs relative to the baseline organization if two conditions hold: contractor wages are lower than government wages *and* the contractor wins the competition. The grade level and step of the position determine government wages. The MEO has no flexibility to pay lower wages for a position in a particular grade level.[10] Thus, even if government wages are lower than contractor wages, and the government wins the competition, reduced wages cannot be a source of savings for the MEO relative to the baseline organization: the cost of a GS-5 will be

---

[10]As discussed earlier, the MEO can lower the wage bill by downgrading positions (replacing workers of a higher grade with workers of a lower grade), civilianizing positions, or reducing the workforce.

the same before and after the cost comparison competition. Both of these conditions held for only one competition: BOS #2.[11]

Capital-Labor Substitution

We anticipated a possibility of substantial personnel savings generated through capital-labor substitution. In addition, we hypothesized that contractors would have an advantage over the in-house organization in terms of their ability to take advantage of opportunities for such substitution. However, we found little capital-labor substitution in either MEO wins or contractor wins.[12]

Several contractor representatives and many functional managers stressed that the options for capital-labor substitution on the part of a contractor are limited because capital use is usually prescribed by the PWS. Although nothing in the competitive process excludes either the MEO or the contractor bid from using additional capital in place of labor, interviewees stressed that the government provides the facilities, equipment, spare parts, and other physical capital, so that the competition tends to be over labor costs only. We do not suggest that no opportunities exist for the government to benefit from capital-labor substitution or other nonlabor cost savings.

We observed other minor nonlabor-related sources of savings that came from changes written into the PWS. The MM study consolidated the workload into one facility, reducing facility costs as well as the cost of operating a vehicle that transported workers and equipment. BOS #1 competition generated minor savings by closing a warehouse. The AM #2 competition likely generated significant

---

[11]For a more detailed discussion of the wage comparison and the calculations underlying this result, see Appendix C.

[12]In MEO wins we were able to observe such substitution directly in the PWS, management study, or both. In contractor wins we could rely only on interview responses to examine this issue. In only one study (BOS #1), did the contractor report installing computers io reduce the workload and cut down on labor costs. In this instance, the contractor admitted that the labor savings benefits inherent in substitution were modest. Indeed, when asked about the sources of personnel savings, the contractor mentioned capital-labor substitution only when probed.

nonlabor savings by consolidating activities onto one installation (but with offsetting transportation costs).[13]

QUESTION 3: ARE THE SAVINGS REAL AND ENDURING?

The magnitude of the estimated expected initial savings suggests that there are in fact positive savings generated by these studies, although we are concerned that the magnitude of the expected savings is overestimated to some degree. The savings also appear to be enduring, but better tracking is needed to be certain of this.

Are the Savings Estimates Real?

The expected personnel cost savings estimates for the competitions we examined are consistent with or exceed expectations based on estimates from previous studies (e.g., Tighe et al., 1996). Given the magnitude of these savings estimates and the fact that the winning bidders did implement their bid, the A-76 savings apparently are real.

Our estimates differ from the standard estimates generated by previous studies by CNA and GAO in two important respects. First, our savings estimates show higher percentages because they consider only personnel costs, and because most if not all of the savings in an A-76 competition are generated through personnel-cost reductions. We emphasize that these personnel cost estimates reflect the savings as a percentage of baseline personnel costs. CNA and GAO studies consider materials and supply costs as well as personnel costs, so their percentage of savings naturally will be lower. Our estimates closely resemble the overall savings estimates in studies with little or no materials and supply costs. However, because our studies do not consider cost of materials or supplies, our percentage estimates will be higher for studies with high materials and supply costs.

---

[13]It is worth noting that any nonlabor savings that are written into the PWS are generally not calculated as cost savings stemming from the A-76 process because they are common to both MEO and contractor wins and thus are not factored into baseline costs. We ignore these savings in our cost estimates; they are usually not significant and are often zero.

A second feature of our analysis is that when calculating baseline costs, we excluded unfilled vacancies at the time of the competition announcement and positions that had already been targeted for elimination. Excluding such positions reduced by the same amount the estimates of baseline personnel cost as well as personnel cost savings, thereby reducing estimated percentage savings.[14] For example, without this adjustment, the estimated cost savings in the MM study would have been 63 percent rather than 59 percent.

However, we have several concerns about the information that is gathered before, during, and after the A-76 competition. These concerns cast doubt on the precision of these cost savings estimates. Although the issues raised herein are not significant enough to shake our confidence in the overall conclusion that A-76 studies do generate substantial personnel cost savings, we believe that the savings estimates could be improved through attention to a number of issues discussed in Appendix D.

Are the Savings Estimates Enduring?

Our analysis suggests that savings persist over time. However, as with the previous question, we believe that data limitations affect the answer to this question. In particular, while it is possible to track whether costs go up or down relative to the initial bid, it is difficult to evaluate whether those changes are appropriate given changes in circumstances.

There is widespread concern that competitions won by contractors are subject to cost escalation. At the same time, the MEO might possibly suffer from cost escalation as well. To explore this issue we examined changes in the cost of the contract over time.

---

[14]The calculation of baseline personnel costs involves estimating the number of people currently performing the function and then estimating the cost of those personnel. This calculation would appear to be fairly straightforward. However, we noticed a strong tendency on the part of installations to make the estimate of baseline personnel costs as large as possible in order to create the appearance of more substantial savings. Several of the cost comparison studies provided three types of personnel lists: authorized, actual, and MEO. Whenever possible, we used the *actual* personnel to estimate the baseline costs, although the installations (and hence the CAMIS database) generally used the *authorized* personnel to calculate the baseline if that number was larger.

Table 3.2

Difference Between Contractor Bid and Actual Contract Payment

Function	Performance Period	Cost Change (%)	Reason
BOS #2	1	+ 1.5	Work performed over and
	2	+ 3.4	above normal duty hours
	Total: 1 and 2	+ 2.5	
AM #2	1	No change	
	2		
TEL	1	− 13	Contract line items deleted due to declining workload

Analysis of Changes in Contract Cost and MEO Staffing

Changes in the contract price over time for contractor wins are displayed in Table 3.2. One performance period is one year in duration. Thus, for the BOS #2 and AM #2 studies we report the change in contract price over two years; for the TEL competition we report the change over one year. Changes in the number of authorized positions for the MEO for in-house wins are displayed in Table 3.3.[15] In calculating the escalation in contract costs, we included only additional payments to the contractor for services rendered, not additional payments to reimburse the contractor for supplies required to perform the function. Also note that these estimates do not include changes in the cost to the government of monitoring and administering the contract.

Tables 3.1 and 3.2 do not suggest a major difference between contractor wins and in-house wins. Within each set of results, we witness one cost or billet increase, one decrease, and one instance of no change. Under both scenarios, cost or authorization increases or decreases are concurrent with changes in mission. The cost reduction in TEL clearly stems from the services being in the process of closing the function at that location. By the end of the first performance period, several line items had been deleted from the contract, and more

---

[15]As noted earlier, no information was available on the cost of an implemented MEO.

Table 3.3

Difference Between Personnel Slots in MEO Bid and Current Staffing

Function	Performance Period	Authorization Change	Reason
BOS #1	Net change, July 1994 to July 1998	+ 4% overall plus upgraded eight WG-2 and four WG-3 positions to WG-5	Overall mission change: increase in student load (the organization's primary mission is technical training)
			Civil Engineering: + 26% due to expanded mission (increase in the number of students). Positions upgraded because initial job descriptions were inadequate
			Supply: – 8% due to closing the supply shop
			Transportation: + 9.3% due to expanded mission
			MWR: – 10%
			Telephone: + 40%. Added two GS-3 positions and upgraded one GS-5 position to a GS-6. MEO did not account adequately for absences.
AM #1	Net change April 1989 to July 1998	– 10%	Authorizations are linked to flight hours by a formula stipulated in the MEO plan. The responsible major command monitors authorizations according to this formula and has adjusted, added, or deleted authorizations eight times.
MM	October 1997 to September 1998	No change	Current authorizations reflect MEO bid.

were slated for removal in the second performance period. Similarly, in AM #1, the number of personnel authorizations was controlled by the responsible major command, which had linked the number of authorizations required to the expected number of flying hours at that particular installation. However, while the total number of authorizations was monitored rather closely, apparently the grade level of those authorizations or the cost of personnel filling those billets received no special scrutiny. They were monitored no more closely than similar changes in authorizations for non-MEO activities.

Both BOS #1 and BOS #2 exhibit some cost increase. In the case of BOS #2, there is a clear cost increase: an addition to the contract for "over and above work" outside of normal duty hours. This work, for one reason or another, does not appear in the contract. With BOS #1, this situation is complicated by an increase in mission (student load) at the installation leading to an increase in the workload. However, it is also clear that some of the changes, such as upgrading the WG-2 and WG-3 positions, are not caused by mission changes. Even the increase in the telephone operator function appears to result from a simple underestimate of the number of people required to do the work, rather than an increase in mission.

Endurance of Savings is Difficult to Track

The analysis presented in the previous section provided no clear evidence of large-scale cost escalation. In spite of this, we hesitate to conclude that cost escalation does not exist. We consider several issues. First, tracing changes in cost to changes in mission is often difficult. Second, the cost of the MEO is not well tracked. Finally, the government does not track changes in the cost of monitoring contracts.

- *Changes in cost versus changes in mission.* The cost of performing a service is clearly related to the level of work required. Cost comparison competitions are conducted at a specific point in time. While they often try to account for possible or even anticipated changes in workload, anticipating all possible contingencies in a contract or MEO is impossible. Regardless of whether changes are anticipated, changes in mission will generate changes in the cost of performing the service. These changes raise challenges in evaluating the information on cost escalation for a contract or an MEO. In both BOS competitions, there were increases in cost or authorizations that were explained by changes in mission on those installations. However, the question remains as to whether the increase in cost was appropriate given the change in mission. Because the mission change was not tracked in a concrete way and because there was no formal link between "mission" and costs, it is not possible to evaluate the appropriateness of those increases. We describe some of the mission changes we observed in our site visits and the possible cost implications of those changes.

The BOS #1 case illustrates some of the concerns in this area. This installation provides training courses for military personnel. These courses have recently been opened to personnel in other services, generating an increase in the average daily student load. This increase led to the addition of eight authorizations in CE, two in the transportation function, and two in the telephone operator area. Interestingly, the MWR billeting function witnessed a decrease in personnel during this same period.

The concerns are similar, but perhaps more subtle, when there are decreases in mission. When missions contract, the cost of providing support services should decline over time. The question is whether the decline in costs is appropriate given the decline in mission. This issue is particularly important to consider because most of these studies were being implemented in a period of overall downsizing within DoD. Thus, the fact that we have not observed much contract cost escalation in this environment does not imply that cost escalation will not occur in the future. Had the original scope of work been maintained, the TEL contract likely would have experienced a cost increase of between 5 and 10 percent in the second year due to the unionization of the workforce.[16] However, because workload had declined so much in the major command responsible for the function, the activity was being phased out at that location, contract line items were eliminated, and there was an overall reduction in the cost of the contract.

---

[16]In this study, the contractor's workforce was unionized within six months of the start of the contract. The contractor petitioned for those wage increases to be covered immediately, but the government denied the request, stating that if it occurred so quickly, then the contractor should have known that it would happen and should have written those wage levels into the contract bid. Thus, the government determined that it would begin covering the cost of the wage increase starting in the first option period (the second year of the contract). The union agreement increased wages by 10 percent and the government is responsible only for the direct costs associated with that wage increase. There is no overhead rate or contract fee applied to this amount.

In the BOS #2 competition, the installation was gaining mission in some areas and downsizing in others, and determining the overall impact of these two forces on BOS workload was difficult. Moreover, the installation expanded the scope of work in the contract to include the supply purchase function, which was not part of the original contract.

Both AM competitions used flying hours by aircraft in supported organizations as measures of mission-related demand. For the AM #1 MEO, the number of manpower authorizations was adjusted (both upward and downward) several times in response to flying-hour fluctuations. In addition, for the first several years after implementation, the command had a "no grade increase without a grade decrease" policy so that the grade level of the authorizations was also more-or-less fixed. This policy indirectly controlled the costs of this MEO. In spite of this policy, however, the civilian personnel officer noted some grade creep over time in the years after this restriction was relaxed. Payments for the AM #2 contract are similarly tied to flying hours.

- *Tracking the cost of an MEO.* Our second concern is that once the cost comparison study is over, the government does not appear to treat an MEO differently from any other function; the manpower office or service command continues to monitor the number of authorizations but not the cost of filling those authorizations. No installation was able to provide us with a cost estimate of the current staffing for the function. One civilian personnel officer said, "We should produce information that way, but we don't." This CPO reported that the only cost estimate available for individual functions would simply take the number of authorizations and multiply that by the base-wide composite rate: the installation-wide average personnel cost.

While there was a general sense among functional managers and installation manpower officials that the cost of the MEO was being monitored, no one was able to identify who was doing the monitoring. An installation manpower official for the BOS #1 competition viewed it as his personal responsibility to ensure that the MEO targets were being met. He suggested that the losing contractors might look at the MEO costs and complain if they saw the costs going up. However, we saw no evidence of this review and complaint occurring.

In the MM competition, there had been no change in the number of authorizations over the life of the MEO and current staffing reflected the number of authorizations. However, the functional manager said that he was expecting a cut because workload was declining. Because missile maintenance occurs through an interservice support agreement (ISSA), the customer organization has some incentive to monitor MEO costs.

Although authorizations are a good proxy for personnel costs, the two may not be directly linked. Costs may not track authorizations because of problems with staffing—inability to fill authorizations completely or in a timely way. Staffing is clearly a challenge for the MEOs. Ironically, this difficulty might improve the government's cost performance in the short run by holding down labor costs; however, it might also lead to problems with MEO development in the future. With the general downsizing of the workforce in DoD, many commands have imposed personnel restrictions on installations, such as hiring freezes and mandatory personnel cuts. In addition, installations must consider filling a vacant position through the priority placement program (PPP), or "stopper list," before they can hire someone outside of DoD for a vacant position. Several of the functional managers and local civilian personnel officials we spoke with said that the recent regionalization of civilian personnel staffing functions has exacerbated delays in the staffing process.[17] They stressed that such delays become extremely important when the MEO wins a competition that had been staffed with a substantial number of military personnel because new civil service workers must be hired to fill those military positions. They also mentioned that staffing delays create problems for functions with high turnover rates or functions that are located at bases undergoing a major downsizing.

---

[17]We note that staffing problems attributed to regionalization may be transitional or may be related to understaffing of regional activities. Tracing the cause of these problems was beyond the scope of this study.

Another reason that costs might not track authorizations is that the cost of a person filling a position may not equal the cost projected in the MEO bid. Although it is possible that some new hires would, for a time, be less costly than the composite costs used in pricing the MEO, a number of factors tend to push actual costs above composite levels. This increase would occur if the individual filling the position benefited from retained higher grade or pay following a reduction in force (RIF). RIFed employees could become part of the workforce either through local bumping and retreating or through the PPP if they are eligible for a position in the MEO under such policies.

- *Contract monitoring costs.* A-76 provisions place an upper limit on the contract administration costs that can be included in the cost comparison study. The number of allowable contract administration personnel is directly linked to the number of workyears in the MEO bid. For example, if the MEO staffing was 100, a maximum of four full-time equivalents (FTE) can be included in the cost of contract administration. We found that there was often a disconnect between the estimated and actual contract monitoring costs. We observed substantial variation among the contractor wins in the costs of monitoring and administering the contracts. Although there were differences in the size and complexity of the contracted activities, the size of the activity alone does not appear to explain all the differences. We believe that the government would benefit from a more careful tracking of contract administration and monitoring costs, associating variation with function, contract features, and the size of the function.

Several interviewees noted substantial problems administering the BOS #2 contract. Consequently, the number of Quality Assurance Evaluators (QAEs) has been increased from seven to 11 and the number of full-time contracting officers and administrators from one to three. According to many involved, the problems are multifaceted and stem from an inadequate PWS (which was based on a command template and was not well suited to the installation), the contract structure (firm, fixed price contract), and a generally adversarial relationship between the government and the contractor. The contracting officer mentioned several times that she felt like her hands were tied because a contractor was living up to the (albeit inadequate) PWS. According to the contracting officer, the firm fixed price contract does not provide a carrot (to motivate good performance) or stick (to punish poor performance). Although in theory the commander could choose not to renew the contract, this is in fact very hard to do without a record of contract discrepancy reports and documentation of established trends of failure to perform. Additionally, recompeting the contract takes a long time, and there is a risk that the contractor's performance would deteriorate further while the installation waited for the new contractor. Apparently, the impact of a past performance report on future contract selections has the strongest impact on the contractor's current performance.

The variation in the amount of time devoted to contract monitoring is driven home by a comparison with the TEL case. In the latter case are one local contracting officer's representative (who is also working as the contracting officer's representative (COR) for several other contracts in the command) and a contracting officer in the regional office who administers this contract in addition to several others. The contracting officer reports spending "nowhere near one FTE" administering this contract and attributes this efficiency to the good relationship between the government and this contractor. Both want to see things go as smoothly as possible. The contracting officer's representative explained the situation in the following way: Only a handful of companies exist that can perform this sort of work for the government. Because the government expects to let more contracts and recompete old contracts in this area in the near future, the contractor places a high value on its past performance rating. Therefore, the contractor is willing to go beyond the letter of the contract as long as it is not too costly.

The AM #2 contract was also creating contract administration problems because the PWS, while accounting for possible changes in mission, did not take into account possible changes in workload mix. The AM #2 function involves two types of service: scheduled overhaul and unscheduled maintenance. The contract is pegged to the number of flying hours and uses historical trends to determine how many scheduled and unscheduled repairs will be needed. The contractor receives a certain amount per unit serviced, regardless of the type. However, the number of unscheduled repairs has been declining and the difficulty of those that remain has increased. This command has consolidated aircraft repair in regional centers. The consolidation has generated a change in the composition of the workload because other installations tend not to ship components to this regional activity for minor repairs that can be performed locally. As a result, the average cost per repair exceeds the target cost. Another problem is that the government is having a supply problem, and the contractor is being forced to cannibalize other aircraft for parts in order to complete the repairs.

QUESTION 4: COULD THE COST SAVINGS BE ACHIEVED OUTSIDE THE A-76 PROCESS?

In the course of this study, we uncovered no obvious strategy that would allow DoD to reap the savings achieved through the A-76 process through other means. In order to promote reengineering broadly, DoD would need to institute comprehensive reforms aimed at shifting the incentives for efficiency improvement currently faced by managers.

Avenues Exist for Government Managers to Make Cost Saving Changes

When we embarked upon this study we anticipated that we might find specific rules or regulations that prevent government managers from making cost-saving changes and that ultimately put the government at a disadvantage in cost comparison studies. We found no such barriers. The government can take advantage of a wide array of savings opportunities including multiskilling, downgrading positions, and organizational streamlining. The only cost-saving technique that is unavailable to the government is paying lower wages, but that does not seem to be an extremely important source of savings.

Government Managers Are Discouraged from Pursuing Savings

Our interviews indicate that A-76 competitions are needed to provoke such efficiency improvements. Without the credible threat of outsourcing, there are few incentives to find and implement workforce cost reductions. At the same time, managers face numerous disincentives that deter them from doing so—they suffer some direct burden if they do it.

In the private sector, managers face strong incentives to improve efficiency and effectiveness. The quality of the output and the cost of generating that output are monitored and the manager is evaluated on the basis of that cost and quality, among other things. If a manager identifies a way to produce the same quality output at less cost, he or she may get a bonus, a raise, or a promotion. At the same time, a manager who is unable to control costs and quality, or does not seek out opportunities to reduce costs, could be fired if such cost-cutting is expected.

Government managers are often not evaluated on organizational outputs or outcomes because outcomes are too difficult to measure or because they depend on factors beyond the managers' control. If managers are judged on outputs or outcomes, such evaluations tend to be based on quality but not cost. With such incentives, managers tend to maximize the availability of resources—including human resources—required to produce quality outputs. At the same time, government managers face virtually no threat of being fired for a failure to control cost. One civilian personnel officer noted that there is no reason that government managers could not be evaluated and promoted on a cost-effectiveness basis; they simply are not. Most managers we spoke with reported that they did not think about these issues until the A-76 competition began. Even when faced with the competitive threat posed by an A-76 competition, many managers still resisted. For example, the manpower officer of the BOS #1 study noted that some managers resisted cutting or downgrading positions. These behaviors are consistent with economic perspective on public choice. Niskanen (1971) argues that bureaucrats maximize their own self-interest (salary, perquisites of office, public reputation, power, and patronage) by maximizing the size of their agencies.

This behavior is consistent with incentives that work against managerial efforts to cut costs or streamline the workforce. As discussed above, OSD, Military Departments and Defense Agencies tend to control costs by controlling authorizations. This control process is often remote and slow to react to changing circumstances, and may be applied in an across-the-board manner that does not take into account local conditions or past performance improvements. Why should a manager volunteer to cut staff or budget if prior cost-cutting actions are not considered when across-the-board budget cuts (e.g., base-wide or command-wide) are instituted? Further, in the event that workload increases, managers may not be able to obtain additional authorizations, much less additional employees, for quite some time. This condition creates incentives for managers to hoard labor (or at least authorizations) for fear of being shorthanded if workload increases or authorizations are cut. This fear becomes all the more salient when a hiring freeze is in effect.

Another important factor discouraging personnel cost-cutting is the human element of the streamlining process. As we have seen, performing a function at lower cost generally means performing the function with fewer people. One manpower officer noted the difficulty of cutting an authorization because of the potential impact on the affected person in terms of lost salary and retirement benefits, etc. Managers have a very difficult time with this problem. Streamlining the workforce also means that the remaining workers may have to work harder. In two of the three MEOs, workers were extremely resentful of the changes brought about by the MEO and were filing numerous grievances through their union.

The A-76 competitive process essentially corners managers into making these tough decisions. The choice is no longer between the relatively comfortable status quo and a more streamlined organization, but between that streamlined organization and outsourcing. As one manpower officer stressed to the functional managers in charge of developing the MEO, if they do not submit a lean bid, they and everyone else would lose their jobs. Even with such a dismal possibility facing them, the functional managers were reluctant to pursue savings aggressively. In one study, won by a contractor, the in-house workforce was confident that the MEO would win the bid because the in-house workforce had won other competitions at that installation. Some people involved in the MEO development suggested that complacent managers did not cut as much as they could have in the MEO.

However, even when there is a threat of losing a large number of jobs, getting employees to accept necessary changes can be difficult. In two MEO wins, managers complained that they got support for certain changes (organizational restructuring, multiskilling) from the union and the workforce. However, once the study was over and the MEO was implemented, the union again became hostile to the MEO. At BOS #1, grievances had been filed over "changes in working conditions" because multiskilling led to a more intense work pace. At MM, workers were petitioning for grade increases and complaining that there were now so few WG-13 positions that they saw little hope of a promotion. The union at MM distrusts management and has suggested that the managers have attempted to reduce authorizations to a level that would allow them to outsource the function under a direct conversion. We observed nothing in MM that suggested managers were interested in such outsourcing.

Government Managers Are Often Not Trained to Identify and Implement Savings

We also found some indication that managers are not properly trained to identify and implement cost-saving changes. One functional manager who provided key input into the PWS and MEO of the TEL study stressed that it is difficult to get managers to think "outside the box." Many of these people have been doing things the same way for up to 20 years. Over this time, they have perceived their primary obligation as following the rules and regulations. When faced with a task such as developing an MEO, they find it difficult to think about how to change the process.

The functional manager for the MM study echoed this sentiment, noting that many managers of service functions started as regular workers and have been promoted through the functional ranks into supervisory positions. Often they are promoted for reasons, such as seniority or technical expertise, that have little to do with their managerial abilities and potential. Many are less than fully prepared to be good managers. The MM functional manager said that available management-training programs tend to focus on bureaucratic procedures (e.g., how to fill out a particular form used in the A-76 process), not on ways to improve efficiency or manage people. He suggested that workforce productivity could benefit from a more broad-based management-training program.

"Come as You Are" Competition

The A-76 process leads to productivity improvement by eliminating the current way of doing business as a credible option. Competition forces managers to improve efficiency or risk losing their (and everyone else's) job. While any change to the existing system would require an in-depth analysis considering the potential intentional and unintentional effects, it is worthwhile to consider whether other, more efficient ways to eliminate the current way of doing business might exist as a viable choice for managers.

For example, one inefficiency of the current A-76 program is that its impact is limited to activities identified for cost comparison studies. A-76 incentives could be broadened to all DoD commercial activities, not just those identified for study, if activities were required to compete on a "come as you are" basis. The organization in place at the time a study is announced would compete against the best private-sector bid.

This approach would be even more effective if it targeted in-house activities that made the least efficiency gains. Such an approach would amplify the incentive to improve efficiency: activities that make themselves more efficient would not only fare better if eventually competed, they also would face a lower probability of having to undergo an A-76 competition in the first place. Additionally, competitions focused on the least efficient in-house activities might yield greater savings than competitions involving more efficient in-house activities.

The success of these efforts would depend on the services' and agencies' abilities to identify the least efficient organizations—in other words, the existence of productivity measures. In cases where the government could not identify satisfactory measures of productivity, such a selection policy would penalize organizations that were already operating more efficiently before the implementation of the policy.

Another important limitation of this approach is that activities that face a *possible* competition at some future time would have less incentive to organize efficiently than activities facing imminent competition under current policy. Nonetheless, when *all* in-house commercial activities face a weaker incentive to become efficient, the savings might be greater than when only a subset of commercial activities, identified for A-76 studies, face a somewhat stronger incentive.

To make themselves more competitive on a "come as you are" basis, each in-house commercial activity would have to reengineer in ways similar to those identified while developing an MEO for an A-76 competition.[18] Although long-run savings would be expected, these reengineering efforts are expensive in the short run. Many DoD organizations may not have the resources or skills needed to reengineer all of their commercial activities in the near term. Moreover, such a policy might be viewed as incompatible with the spirit of A-76, which gives government employees the right to compete with the private sector to provide a good or service. Finally, in the absence of imminent competition, functional managers within higher headquarters staffs might be unwilling to permit the kinds of cross-functional reorganization and multitasking that often contribute significantly to the efficiencies found in MEOs. Thus, additional analysis would be required to assess the fairness and feasibility of using "come as you are" competitions.

---

[18]Such reengineering could include efforts to restructure or regroup different functions or to change the scope of work.

strong structural incentives in place that deter managers from making such changes if they are not involved in an A-76 competition. An A-76 competition fundamentally changes the choices available to managers. Rather than comparing potentially painful reforms to the status quo, the manager must compare those reforms to the possibility of the entire function being outsourced. Competition, or more precisely the credible threat of losing everything in the competitive process, induces managers to make efficiency-enhancing changes they might otherwise resist. We conclude that comprehensive reforms, reducing the negative incentives and improving the positive incentives, would be needed to encourage DoD managers to reduce personnel costs voluntarily. In addition, training is needed to assist functional managers in identifying and implementing personnel cost savings opportunities.

TRADE-OFFS ARE INHERENT IN MANY PERSONNEL MANAGEMENT POLICIES AND PRACTICES

Management of the DoD civil service workforce is controlled by a variety of rules, regulations, policies, and practices from several entities, including Congress, OMB, OPM, OSD, and the components. Many rules are well-intended and help the entity in question achieve important goals. For example:

- The PPP reflects a commitment to current workers that might make DoD civil service more attractive to prospective workers and help maintain morale during a general downsizing.

- Veterans' hiring preferences make military service more attractive and represent a form of social payback to individuals who have made personal sacrifices to provide for the common defense of the nation.

- A centralized examining and certification process, run by OPM for most initial competitive appointments in the civil service, assures fairness and consistency in federal hiring practices.[1]

- Classification policies for multiskilled positions promote comparable pay for comparable work.

---

[1] In some cases, OPM delegates examining authority to agencies.

At the same time, many policies and procedures have important efficiency implications. These programs may introduce delays in hiring or result in the hiring of workers who are less qualified or more expensive than others in the available pool. We see no way to eliminate these trade-offs. We would like to point out, however, that such trade-offs will tend to have a more significant impact on more efficient, streamlined organizations with little or no slack resources than in other areas. In view of such consequences, it might be important to review current policies in terms of their compatibility with DoD's initiatives to create high-efficiency, high-performance organizations.

POLICY RECOMMENDATIONS

The A-76 process generates a wealth of knowledge regarding how to improve efficiency in government-run organizations. Many functional areas, particularly inherently governmental activities, could benefit from the exchange of information on cost-saving techniques. The methods through which savings are achieved could be documented and disseminated DoD-wide. However, the exchange of information is not sufficient to promote efficiency-enhancing changes.

Improving Efficiency Without Competition

Several reforms to DoD's internal management system would be required to generate personnel cost savings outside the A-76 process. First, OSD, Military Departments, and Defense Agencies need to provide more positive incentives to local commanders and managers. Local commanders and local functional managers have the detailed process knowledge required to identify opportunities for cost savings. They also face the strongest disincentives to undertake change. To improve this scenario, DoD could turn to both individual and organizational rewards. DoD performance evaluations could explicitly consider the extent to which managers have identified and implemented cost savings. Managers and their workforces also could have a real opportunity to earn performance, gainsharing, or goalsharing bonuses for their cost-saving efforts.[2] Additionally, organizations

---

[2]Gainsharing bonuses are sometimes used as an incentive for a workforce to reduce the costs of production. In a gainsharing plan, costs of production are periodically

might be permitted to apply a portion of savings toward other (unfunded) needs.

Functional managers at service and major command headquarters also play a key role in making operations more efficient. These managers often have a significant voice in both the design of processes used locally and in resourcing local operations. Because of these roles, headquarters functional managers may in some cases have more impact on the efficiency of local operations than local commanders and managers. Compared to local commanders and managers, headquarters functional managers are more likely to be confronted with competing demands, and therefore more likely to seek the kind of efficiencies that would stretch scarce resources so as to meet as many demands as possible. However, like local commanders and managers, headquarters staffs have little or no incentive to reduce the overall level of resourcing in their function. Thus, considering performance, gainsharing, or goalsharing bonuses for these staffs might also be useful.[3]

To ensure that mission support would not be inappropriately sacrificed for personal gain, any such system of incentives would require clear and measurable organizational performance benchmarks that encompass the most important organizational outputs and outcomes. These outputs and outcomes would have to be routinely measured. Additionally, legislation might be necessary to implement bonus systems that are large enough to provide the necessary incentives and can be applied equally to military and civilian members of the workforce. In devising such a system, forethought would be required to ensure that costs of the measurement and incentive systems do not exceed the expected efficiency gains.

---

compared to expected costs and a portion of the difference is returned to workers in the form of a bonus. When costs of production are difficult to track, as in many public-sector organizations, a variant called goalsharing is sometimes used. In this variant, bonuses are awarded to the workforce whenever an activity meets a substantial proportion of predetermined performance goals.

[3]Baldwin et al. (1998) discuss a related topic, namely the incentives encountered by Air Force employees at many levels of the organization to initiate A-76 competitions. They argue that the incentives facing the installation-level functional managers and commanders tend to work against A-76 efforts promoted by the major commands.

A second and more difficult task is to eliminate negative incentives inhibiting efficiency-enhancing changes. Many of these stem from long-standing DoD management practices. In the current environment, managers resist streamlining the workforce because keeping an organization fully staffed is difficult. In addition, they fear that when future budget and personnel cuts are implemented, their previous cost-cutting efforts will not be acknowledged and they will face the same across-the-board cuts as everyone else. These are real concerns for managers.

In terms of staffing, OSD, Military Departments and Defense Agencies might be able to provide a more encouraging environment for reform by streamlining staffing procedures for highly efficient organizations, exempting them from installation hiring freezes, or by giving them staffing priority in the event that a position becomes vacant during a time when there are hiring restrictions placed on installations. Such functions also might be exempted from across-the-board budget and manpower cuts for a specific period of time unless there were a change in mission or demonstrable inefficiencies in the function. Such an arrangement would require effective metrics to identify efficient and inefficient organizations. Furthermore, such metrics would have to be accessible to both installation-level commanders and higher-headquarters functional managers, since either or both might play a role in allocating arbitrary cuts.

Finally, competition-related incentives can be extended immediately and continuously to all commercial organizations by requiring them to compete on a "come as you are" basis in A-76 cost comparison competitions. Although there are some negatives associated with this approach, it warrants further study.

While providing managers with positive incentives and removing negative incentives is crucial, it is also important that front-line managers receive training and support that enable them to undertake such reforms. Our interviews suggested that civilian front-line managers, who tend to be promoted into supervisory positions through functional ranks, do not necessarily receive training in management-related skills comparable to the leadership and management training incorporated in officer and enlisted professional military education courses. Documenting and disseminating information on cost-saving initiatives throughout DoD may be important, but these cannot replace broader training and education of functional managers.

Better Data Are Needed to Support High-Level Decisionmaking

In spite of the emphasis being placed on the A-76 process as a method to generate cost savings, the data on which high-level decisions (such as budget cuts) are currently being made have many problems. Existing estimates of savings from our case studies are hampered by a lack of guidance on calculating baseline costs and a lack of good accounting of the costs of support activities before or after the implementation of a more efficient organizational form.

DoD must improve the quality of the information to determine how much it will actually save, how much it will cost installations to perform competitions, and which activities generate the most savings. In particular, it is important to evaluate cost savings from the perspective of DoD as a whole, as opposed to narrowly defined activities subject to A-76 competition. In defining the scope of the cost analysis too narrowly, costs that are incurred outside the entity under scrutiny, yet still borne by DoD, are easily overlooked. For example, little or no information currently is available on the costs of conducting a competition or implementing A-76 results, including contract monitoring.

Ad hoc features of the A-76 process make estimating savings more difficult. For example, as of 1996, OMB has required government agencies involved in A-76 competitions to add 12 percent of direct labor costs (including fringe) to the in-house bid to reflect indirect costs, specifically operations overhead and general and administrative overhead. However, to the extent that this 12 percent overhead is viewed as a real cost that must be included in the cost comparison competition, we would argue that it should also be included when calculating the costs of the baseline organization and the cost of monitoring the contract. This 12 percent rate is completely arbitrary and does not appear to reflect the extent to which overhead costs actually vary with the number of personnel employed.

Consistent, high-quality information on cost savings and other outcomes of the A-76 process will allow OSD, Military Departments, and Defense Agencies to make better decisions about the future implementation of the process—the kinds of savings that can be expected, the time frame during which they can be expected, and the activities that should be targeted. Better information requires precise definitions of terms like *baseline cost* and *cost savings* that are consistent across installations and services. In addition, the government must gather information on the cost of conducting the competitions and continue to collect cost information during the implementation phase of the contract or MEO. In late 1999, the Deputy Under Secretary of Defense for Installations issued new CAMIS procedural guidance that addressed many of these issues (Yim, 1999).

New Approaches to Managing the MEO

OSD, Military Departments, and Defense Agencies also should think about the procedures in place for managing MEOs. It is telling that none of the managers of MEO wins could provide us with cost information—only personnel authorization information. During the A-76 process, the organization is treated like a separate entity and asked to develop a most efficient organizational form—an entity that can provide a specified level of service at the lowest possible cost. However, once the competition is over, no system exists to monitor these organizations and their fulfillment of the MEO. Managers should be given tools to monitor and manage their costs, freedom from additional constraints on the number of personnel authorizations, and other abilities. Similarly, DoD should consider giving MEO managers more control over the staffing of their organizations: The use of the PPP could be expedited for MEOs, and they could be exempt from on-base hiring restrictions for some period after implementation.

SITE VISITS AND INTERVIEW PROTOCOLS

This appendix includes a description of the interviews we conducted at each site (Table A.1) and our interview protocol.

INTERVIEW PROTOCOL

Information to Be Gathered Prior to the Site Visit

Point of contact will be asked to provide advance copies of the following documents regarding the subject activity:

- performance work statement

- MEO documentation

- grade distribution (authorized and assigned) of the workforce prior to the A-76 competition and, if an MEO is in effect, current distribution

- A-76 cost comparison documents

- solicitation/contract file (SF 1447 with attachments, exhibits, revisions, and modifications)

Interviews/Courtesy Calls

1. Senior- and intermediate-level commanders/managers

Introduction

Identify sponsor and explain purpose of project

Table A.1

Description of Site Visit Interviews

Agency/official	Duration	Interview Topics
Senior-level (O-6) commander or staff manager responsible for outsourced activity or MEO	15 minutes	courtesy call
Intermediate-level (O-5) commander or staff manager responsible for outsourced activity or MEO	15 minutes	courtesy call
Manager of the in-house function directly responsible for oversight of the outsourced activity or MEO	1.5 hours	• preparation of the PWS/contract solicitation • latitude to use workforce efficiencies (multiskilling, flattened organization, variable pay, etc.) with a civil service workforce • costs of performing the A-76 competition • contract officers technical representative (COTR), quality assurance, and other oversight responsibilities
Manpower office	1 hour	• conduct of the A-76 competition • size/grade distribution of the pre–A-76 workforce • size/grade distribution of the MEO, if applicable
Government contracting office	1 hour	• basis of the contract awards (low cost/best value) • labor costs, labor force size, and other workforce information available from contractor • contract modifications and cost changes (if any) and reasons for the changes

Table A.1 (continued)

Agency/official	Duration	Interview Topics
Contractor's local manager (only for competitions won by the contractor)	1 hour	• labor force size and cost • use of workforce efficiencies (multiskilling, flattened organization, variable pay) • contract modifications and reasons for
Civilian personnel office	1 hour	• relative in-house versus contractor workforce size and cost • latitude to use workforce efficiencies (multiskilling, flattened organization, variable pay) with a civil service workforce
Civil service employee union representative	30 minutes	• union perspective on workforce efficiencies (multiskilling, flattened organization, variable pay)

Outline issues being explored and personnel being contacted

Provide assurance of nonattribution/anonymity of sites visited

Offer copy of final report. If interested, address to: _____

In general, how comfortable are you with the outsourcing/MEO arrangement? What were the primary benefits of this commercial activities process? What were the primary costs of this process?

2. In-house function directly responsible for oversight of the outsourced activity or MEO

Introduction

Identify sponsor and explain purpose of project

Outline issues being explored and personnel being contacted

Provide assurance of nonattribution/anonymity of sites visited

Offer copy of final report. If interested, address to: _____

Preparation of the PWS

- Who prepared PWS? Was there any input from the command, service, or OSD (e.g., a template, a "tiger team")?

- Was the preparation team experienced?

- Did the PWS adequately describe the requirement? If not, what was the nature of the deficiency?

- Were subsequent contract modifications needed? If so, were they due to deficiencies in the PWS or to other reasons (e.g., changes in DoD requirements, changes in DoL wage rates)?

Conduct of the A-76 competition

- Did stakeholders (workers, managers) consider the process fair?

- Who prepared the MEO bid? Was there input from the command, service, or OSD?

- How was the MEO labor estimate developed? Did the MEO bid contain enough labor to adequately provide the required service?

- Were in-house and contractor costs accurately accounted for in the competition? In particular, were the costs of monitoring and administering the contract adequately considered?

- What relative advantages led to the contractor/MEO win?

Workforce efficiencies

- How does the contractor/MEO workforce size and composition compare to the pre–A-76 workforce?

- If the activity was contracted out, are there any remaining in-house personnel who monitor or in other ways administer the activity?

- Has the contractor/MEO employed workforce efficiencies (multi-skilling, flattened organization, variable pay, etc.) not commonly available with civil service workforces or not previously used with the in-house workforce?

- Are there specific tasks previously performed by the in-house activity that the contractor/MEO was able to eliminate or perform with less labor?

- Is there any evidence that the contractor/MEO substituted capital for labor?

- Is there any evidence that the contractor/MEO took advantage of economies of scale by combining service to you with service to other customers? In particular, did economies of scale result in greater productivity or a need for fewer managers?

- Is there any evidence that the contractor pays lower wages than the government? Do you have contractor wage information?

- Are there specific civil service rules or DoD/service personnel policies that tend to detract from workforce productivity or efficiency?

Monitoring performance

- In general, how does contractor/MEO performance compare to previous in-house performance?

- How much effort do you invest in monitoring the contractor's/MEO's performance (COTR, QAEs, etc.)?

- Do you incur any other contract administration costs besides these costs?

- Did comparable monitoring costs exist prior to the A-76 competition?

- Were monitoring costs properly reflected in the contract side of the cost comparison?

- Discuss any issues that surfaced during prior review of PWS, MEO documentation, authorized and assigned strengths, A-76 competition, and solicitation/contract file.

- In general, do you have any observations that would help us understand relative in-house and contractor labor costs and efficiencies?

3. Agency responsible for managing the A-76 competition

Introduction

Identify sponsor and explain purpose of project

Outline issues being explored and personnel being contacted

Provide assurance of nonattribution/anonymity of sites visited

Offer copy of final report. If interested, address to: _____

- Are you aware of any distortions, inaccuracies, or weak estimates in any of the cost comparison data?

- Did stakeholders (you, workers, managers, contractors, contracting office) consider the process fair?

- Have you monitored cost changes (including MEO size and composition, if applicable) subsequent to the initial cost comparison? If so, did any of these changes suggest that initial cost comparison data were inaccurate?

- Did you have any role in assisting the MEO team in estimating its labor requirements?

- Were there problems in the PWS or MEO that had to be corrected later through contract modifications? If so, what was the nature of the changes?

- In general, how readily are workforce efficiencies (multiskilling, flattened organization, variable pay, etc.) used to maximize efficiency of the in-house workforce?

- In general, how readily are capital/labor substitutions used to maximize efficiency of the in-house workforce?

- In this specific case, are there tasks previously performed by the in-house activity that the contractor/MEO was able to eliminate or perform with less labor?

- Discuss any issues that surfaced during prior review of PWS, MEO documentation, authorized and assigned strengths, A-76 competition, and solicitation/contract file.

- In general, do you have any observations that would help us understand relative in-house and contractor labor costs and efficiencies?

4. Contracting office

Introduction

Identify sponsor and explain purpose of project

Outline issues being explored and personnel being contacted

Provide assurance of nonattribution/anonymity of sites visited

Offer copy of final report. If interested, address to: _____

- How did the basis of the contract award (low cost, best value) in-fluence the outcome? Would best value tend to favor contractors or the in-house workforce?

- What kind of information can we get regarding the cost and composition of the contractor's workforce at various points during the performance period?

- Have there been significant contract modifications/cost changes during the performance period? If so, to what do you attribute them? Faulty PWS? Change in demand for services?

- Discuss any issues that surfaced during prior review of PWS, MEO documentation, authorized and assigned strengths, A-76 competition, and solicitation/contract file.

5. Contractor's local manager

Introduction

Identify sponsor and explain purpose of project

Outline issues being explored and personnel being contacted

Provide assurance of non-attribution/anonymity of sites visited

Offer copy of final report. If interested, address to: _____

- How does your workforce size, composition, and cost compare to the pre–A-76 workforce?

- How did you estimate your labor requirement when you submit-ted your bid? Has the requirement changed since then?

- Have you implemented workforce efficiencies (multiskilling, flattened organization, variable pay, etc.) not commonly available with civil service workforces or not previously used with the in-house workforce?

- Are there specific activities previously performed by the in-house activity that you were able to eliminate or perform with less labor?

- Did you substitute capital for labor?

- Did you take advantage of economies of scale, e.g., by combining service to this installation with service to other customers, or by incorporating lessons learned from other sites to this location?

- Discuss any issues that surfaced during prior review of PWS, MEO documentation, authorized and assigned strengths, A-76 competition, and solicitation/contract file.

6. *Civilian personnel office*

Introduction

Identify sponsor and explain purpose of project

Outline issues being explored and personnel being contacted

Provide assurance of nonattribution/anonymity of sites visited

Offer copy of final report. If interested, address to: _____

- Did you have a role in developing the MEO?

- In general, how readily are workforce efficiencies (multiskilling, flattened organization, variable pay, etc.) used to maximize efficiency of the in-house workforce? If these workforce efficiencies are not readily used, is it because of lack of knowledge/interest on the part of local managers, or specific government or DoD constraints?

- In general, how readily are capital/labor substitutions used to maximize efficiency of the in-house workforce?

- Are there specific civil service rules or DoD/service personnel policies that tend to detract from workforce productivity or efficiency?

- Discuss any issues that surfaced during prior review of PWS, MEO documentation, authorized and assigned strengths, A-76 competition, and solicitation/contract file.

- In general, do you have any observations that would help us understand relative in-house and contractor labor costs and efficiencies?

- Do you have any general suggestions as to ways government managers could improve workforce utilization within the constraints of existing civilian personnel policies and procedures?

7. Civil service employee union representatives

Introduction

Identify sponsor and explain purpose of project

Outline issues being explored and personnel being contacted

Provide assurance of nonattribution/anonymity of sites visited

Offer copy of final report. If interested, address to: _____

- From the union's perspective, did the A-76 cost comparison process provide a fair approach for selecting a service provider?

- What is the union's perspective on workforce efficiencies (multiskilling, flattened organization, variable pay, etc.) used to maximize productivity?

- What is the union's perspective on capital/labor substitutions used to maximize productivity?

- Discuss any issues that surfaced during prior review of PWS, MEO documentation, authorized and assigned strengths, A-76 competition, and solicitation/contract file.

- In general, do you have any observations that would help us understand relative in-house and contractor labor costs and efficiencies?

CASE STUDIES

SOURCES OF COST SAVINGS FOR SPECIFIC COMPETITIONS

While it is relatively easy to calculate broad savings estimates on the basis of information contained in cost-comparison documents, an understanding of the sources of those savings can be gleaned only through an in-depth examination of the cases in question. Below, we summarize the sources of cost savings for each of the sites visited. This information was drawn both from the interviews and from document review.

Base Operating Support #1 (BOS #1)

The BOS #1 competition was won by the in-house organization. Most savings were generated by reducing the number of workers required to do the job. This reduction was facilitated primarily by civilianization and organizational restructuring, although multi-skilling also played a minor role. The MEO also generated savings by downgrading positions. Finally, there was some minor capital-labor substitution in the form of installing some computers and reducing the number of workers performing clerical tasks.

The BOS #1 MEO reduced the number of positions by 24 percent and personnel costs by 34 percent. This was a multifunction competition and, as suggested by Table 3.3, the savings varied dramatically across the functions. In each function, the personnel slot savings paralleled personnel cost savings.

The low savings rate in the MWR/billeting function is striking. This is a function that had few military personnel, and even fewer (16 out of 100) appropriated fund (APF) civilians to start with. Moreover, because this was a nonappropriated fund (NAF) function, it was already under pressure to hold down costs (at least the cost of civil service workers).[1] The telephone operator function, which was only five authorizations to begin with, generated no savings. The telephone operator function is an around-the-clock staffing; someone has to be there to answer the phones 24 hours a day, seven days a week. Therefore, the number of people required to fully staff the function is not very flexible.

Savings in this case clearly were achieved by reducing the number of personnel. However, disentangling the changes that allowed for such reduction is difficult.

Civilianization played an important role in reducing the number of supervisors required. All 177 military positions were either eliminated (74) or civilianized (103). The military structure involved a lot of supervision and required hierarchies; for example, the number of squadrons was reduced because the Air Force cannot have a squadron without a commander and the commander has to be a uniformed individual.

In total, 82 percent of the personnel cost savings came from eliminating positions (both civilian and military). Another 18 percent came from direct military-to-civilian conversions.

Other organizational restructuring efforts also played an important role in allowing the reduction in the number of personnel. For example, the logistics group was eliminated and its activities incorporated into other groups. These changes allowed for a reduction in overhead personnel requirements. In addition, the MEO used more

---

[1]Appropriated and nonappropriated funds refer to the source of the funds used to pay the workers. Most civil servants are paid from money that is appropriated by Congress for that purpose. However, there are some services that are supported in whole or in part by user fees. These activities are referred to as NAF activities because they derive at least some of their operating revenue from nonappropriated funds. NAF functions are required to balance their revenue and costs and their workers are covered by a different set of rules and regulations. There is a different pay schedule for NAF employees, a different retirement system and benefit structure, and a less restrictive hiring and firing policy.

work leaders rather than work supervisors,[2] and generally increased the worker/supervisor ratio. For example, one housekeeping superintendent manages 60 positions. In the billeting function, managers have made use of NAF workers, reduced the number of full-time employees, and increased the number of part time employees. Currently, the function has 16 APF workers and the rest are NAF.

The reorganization also generated opportunities for multiskilling. Because the BOS A-76 grouped several independent functions under one umbrella, the managers in the different functional areas came to realize that they could distribute workers across units: workers in supply could be used in transportation and/or CE. The MEO also included limited improvements to the work process. For example, the MEO proposed swing shifts to reduce overtime.

The downgrading of positions is a bit more difficult to understand because it is intermingled with civilianization. Much of the "downgrading" occurred by eliminating proportionately more of the high-grade military positions and civilianizing proportionately more of the low-grade positions. For example, in the civil engineering area, more of the E-6 to E-8 and officer positions were eliminated, whereas more of the E-3 to E-5 positions were converted. Even when higher-grade military positions were civilianized, they were often downgraded in the process. For example, in the billeting function of MWR, There were E-6, E-5, E-4 and E-3 slots on the billeting desk—all were converted to GS-4 positions.[3] The management study also downgraded a number of civilian positions in all functions. Notably, many WG-5 positions in civil engineering were downgraded to WG-2 and WG-3 positions. Collectively, these downgrading actions allowed cost savings to reach 34 percent even though the number of billets was reduced by only 24 percent.

Work scope issues in BOS #1 were not considered in the PWS or management study. However, the base commander noted that be-

---

[2]The advantage of using work leaders is that they can perform both supervisory and functional activities, whereas work supervisors can only engage in supervisory activities.

[3]According to DoD policy, a GS-4 is roughly equivalent to an E-4. In terms of personnel cost of an individual employee, a GS-4 costs more than an E-1, but less than an E-2. However, assessing the cost of a single military or civil service worker is a complicated process. See Gates and Robbert, 1998, for a discussion.

fact convert any slots but simply eliminated all the military positions. The management study of this missile maintenance function argued that the military personnel assigned to this activity were not doing anything related to the function. Some were detailed to drive distinguished visitors around the base, others were on semi-permanent TDY. The MEO development team saw no reason to fill any of the military slots with civilians and simply eliminated the positions.

According to the functional manager, the function had 33 military slots several years before the competition began. At the time of the management study there were 13 military authorizations, only eight of which were actually filled. This accords with staffing information contained in the management study. Moreover, independent of the A-76 competition, several changes were on the horizon for the subsequent year: the elimination of five (of the 13) authorizations (E-5s) and the reassignment of one E-8 authorization to another functional area. In other words, for reasons having nothing to do with the A-76 competition, the number of military personnel assigned to the function was scheduled to decline to seven. The personnel cost savings estimates presented in the management study report calculate the total cost savings based on a reduction from 13 military authorizations. We adjusted the baseline cost estimate to include only those seven authorizations that were scheduled to remain within the function.

On the basis of the estimates used in the management study, the elimination of the military slots accounted for 30 percent of the total personnel cost savings for this function. When we adjusted the baseline personnel cost and personnel cost savings estimates to include only those seven military positions that were staffed and not scheduled for elimination, the civilianization accounted for 19 percent of the total personnel cost savings.

The missile maintenance MEO benefited from organizational restructuring. The most substantial formal change was that the maintenance division was eliminated and the activity placed under the maintenance branch of the equipment management division. No special waivers were required for this change, and it allowed for the elimination of a division chief (E-8) position. Less formal organizational restructuring also occurred. For example, the new organization made more use of wage leader (WL) positions and instituted a quality control system where work leaders could sign off on the work being done. This innovation reduced the number of work supervisors. The MEO reduced the number of supervisors (WS-13) from two to one and the number of wage leaders (WL-13) from five to one. This change accounted for 22 percent of the personnel cost savings.

The management study also reduced costs by altering the grade structure. The changes to grade structure were accomplished through a careful assignment of tasks in the position descriptions. This function is mainly staffed with WG-12 and WG-13 electric integrated systems mechanics. The MEO limited the high grades (WG-13) to the people working on the more complex missile systems that do not have as much self-diagnostic capability and require workers with both electronic and radar expertise. This led to a relatively greater decrease in the number of WG-13 workers. The MEO cut the number of WG-12 workers from 15 to 11, and WG-13 workers from 17 to three.

The civilian personnel officer involved in the A-76 competition noted that part of the reason for the greater-than-proportional cuts in the WG-13 positions stemmed from the fact that the customer organization had phased out its use of one of the two more complex missile systems. She also noted that there were just "too many" high-graded workers. Therefore, it is difficult to determine how much of the grade reduction was due to work mix changes that were occurring during the timeframe of the competition and how much was due to streamlining or modifying position descriptions. Nevertheless, the savings due to these cuts were substantial.

In addition to the changes just discussed, the MEO added a position for a production control clerk, which led to a more efficient organization of the work process. Formerly, there was no system for tracking work and assigning it to workers. Although standard procedures require that a work order be submitted before the work begins, in many cases the supervisors were writing up work orders after the fact. No good record existed of what was being done, and no way to prioritize. Formerly, the function had one GS-5 secretary position. The MEO proposed one GS-5 production support clerk and one GS-7 production control person. The functional manager argued that this position allowed the MEO to operate with fewer mechanics because the organization would be better able to monitor and manage work-load and input requirements.

This streamlining of the core workforce through improved work processes, increased work intensity, and downgrading positions accounted for about 59 percent of the personnel cost savings.

Multiskilling did not appear to be an important source of savings for the MEO relative to the baseline workforce. Several members of the A-76 team reported that the job descriptions for this function have always been flexible, so in some sense there was always multi-skilling. Both before and after, the job descriptions refer to "Electronic Integrated Systems Mechanic," and the management study report makes no explicit mention of multiskilling contributing to the MEO's ability to reduce the number of people employed. These job descriptions allow mechanics to work on all parts of any complicated missile system. From a classification perspective, workers could work on one or several different missile systems. However, in practice workers are assigned to one missile system. The MEO did not change this missile-specific team structure.

The missile maintenance competition also generated some facilities savings that were unrelated to personnel use and were not included in the savings estimates.[4] Consolidating maintenance activities in the facilities of the supported organization allowed the function to vacate 18,721 square feet of space in another building,[5] saving the government about $70,000 per year in base operating support (BOS) costs. The functional manager made the point that BOS "savings" are not really savings since the space is probably just put to another use on the installation. However, they do reflect opportunity costs to the installation. The facility consolidation also allowed the MEO to eliminate one vehicle rental for a savings of about $3000 per year by relocating the direct support maintenance to the building where the missiles are located. These savings are not reported in our savings estimates or in the savings estimates for the A-76 competition.

---

[4]These facilities-related savings were not included in the CAMIS cost savings estimates either. Because the government normally provides facilities to whomever wins the competition, their costs are not generally itemized in the cost-comparison study.

[5]After the study, the function would be assuming only about 10,000 square feet of space.

The missile maintenance function is unique in that it is a service provided by one command for another under an inter-service support agreement (ISSA). The customer organization and the provider organization are in different commands within one service. The customer organization has to budget specifically for the missile maintenance services it purchases from the other organization. Because the customer organization is under budgetary pressure, it is sensitive to the cost of the reimbursement. Among other things, this arrangement seems to create more of an incentive for the customer and the provider to define clearly and look for opportunities to reduce the scope of the work.

The PWS explicitly addressed work scope issues. Some of the work scope adjustments were relatively minor and reflected a new understanding of the division of labor between the customer and the provider organization. During the development of the PWS, the functional manager of the provider organization reviewed the work that was being done and determined that much of the pre-study missile maintenance activity was beyond the scope of the ISSA. For example, individuals from the service provider came in at the start of the day to turn on equipment, although this is something for which the customer is responsible. It was also determined that the customer organization was not living up to some of its preventive maintenance obligations and that this oversight was creating unnecessary work for the provider organization.

Other work scope adjustments were more formal and involved the transfer of authorizations between customer and provider. Workers were doing several things that went beyond the maintenance and support function (e.g., supporting PC users and installing software). The management study determined that this support was not part of the ISSA, and suggested that the function be transferred to the customer organization. The original team performing this activity was composed of a WL and four electronic integrated system mechanics. Three electronic systems mechanic slots were transferred to the customer organization. It appears that when the management study calculated the manpower savings, they included all five positions (including the three that were transferred) in the cost savings. We were told that the customer organization did not actually use the authorizations, but absorbed the workload with its existing workforce, and we were unable to uncover any evidence to the contrary.

Therefore, we included these three authorizations as "savings" in our overall savings estimate.

In summary, the cost savings in the MM competition stemmed from several sources. Civilianization was an important source of savings, as were organizational restructuring and reductions in the scope of work. The consolidation of facilities also contributed to savings.

Base Operating Support #2 (BOS #2)

The BOS #2 competition was won by the contractor. According to the contractor's local manager, the cost savings from this competition came from several different sources: multiskilling, lower wages, organizational restructuring, and increased labor availability.

The contractor hires multiskilled workers and is thereby able to use people across different activities. This flexibility leads to efficiency improvements and allows for the work to be done with fewer workers.[6] Multiskilling facilitated improved work scheduling. In addition, the contractor implemented swing shifts to reduce overtime.

Organizational restructuring and streamlining played an important role in generating cost savings. The contractor has broken down the functional walls between activities and reengineered the work process. This restructuring permitted elimination of several mid-level managers, including three department managers. The contractor anticipates more such reengineering opportunities and may be able to cut even more management personnel.

Because this is the first large government BOS contract for this particular contractor, the participants really do not have any "lessons learned" to apply to this installation. Surprisingly, the contractor said that it shares information on what works with its competitors—

---

[6]One of the QAEs in the facilities area said that the contractor has taken this too far, stating that the contractor "has workers all over the place" in a manner that is well beyond prudent cross-utilization. Clerks are sent to work in the warehouse. The contractor wrote a description for the position of "supply clerk" and got it approved. These clerks can then be sent to work anyplace in the supply function. Government unions would complain if civil servants were assigned to duties outside their occupational boundaries. However, this observer acknowledged that government position descriptions could be written in this way.

not the big national players like Dynacorp, Johnson Control, or Boeing Services, but the smaller regional players. It relocates managers, but not other employees, to other installations or contracts. As managers get more experience, they are moved to larger, more complex contracts.

The contractor reduced labor costs by downgrading positions so that the average grade level is lowered. This downgrade changed the grade mix, reducing the average skill level and wage of the workforce. For example, this BOS contractor uses more general maintenance workers and helpers and fewer journeymen laborers (e.g., carpenters, plumbers, and electricians), who are much more expensive.[7]

The contractor can easily adjust the workforce to respond to changing work volume. The contractor can hire in a few weeks and can fire with minimum due process. Because the contractor does not have to staff for exceptional workloads, staffing can be more streamlined.

The contractor's local representative reported that there was limited opportunity for capital-labor substitution because the equipment usage was prescribed by the PWS. However, the contractor installed additional computers and off-the-shelf software. Computerization freed foremen to be on the job rather than doing paperwork, thereby reducing the total number of workers required.

We found no evidence that the PWS reduced the scope of work in any of the areas studied. However, several people mentioned that the cost comparison process induces one to think about what really needs to be done and what is excessive.

Aircraft Maintenance #2 (AM #2)

The AM #2 competition was won by a contractor. It is difficult to discuss savings generated through this competition because it involved a consolidation of functions from several installations and, as a result, there is no real baseline organization against which to compare

---

[7]One of the government QAEs expressed some concern that the contractor has gone too far with this and that it is leading to high turnover rates.

the contractor. In the end, the contractor bid and the MEO bid were quite close.

The wage differential between the contractor and government was not a substantial factor. As we will discuss later, contractor wages are restricted by the SCA, and in this case these wages are not very different from civil service wages. When we asked the contractor's local manager what his source of advantage was, he noted that the government benefits are much more costly than the contractor's benefits. Another source of advantage for the contractor is a higher manhour availability rate (basically, the number of hours worked per person per year), largely due to less leave time. In addition, the contractor's local manager believes his workers work harder because they are held accountable—they can be fired easily.

We heard conflicting reports on the ability of the contractor to reduce cost by improving the work processes. The function manager who developed the MEO claimed that in the area of aircraft maintenance, neither the contractor nor the MEO has much flexibility to improve work processes because they must follow Air Force regulations and technical orders related to the maintenance process. With all of these process restrictions in place, the government is not really outsourcing the function but rather hiring someone to staff what remains essentially an in-house function.

However, the contractor modified several work processes to generate savings. It streamlined parts flow 20–25 percent by removing needless (and unrequired) processes. In addition, the contractor isolated the tear-down process from the build-up process, thereby removing distractions and improving efficiency. The contractor said that it tended to organize the work more functionally than the task had been under government management. For example, the contractor has three production foremen: one stays with the aircraft, one is in charge of the back shop, and one is in charge of material control. Some of these ideas came from the experience that contractor employees had gained at other installations—usually as military personnel. These individuals based their bid on intimate knowledge of the process.

Telecommunications Operations and Maintenance (TEL)

The TEL competition was won by a contractor after an appeal of the initial decision which was for the in-house organization. Savings from the TEL competition came from several sources, including reduced work scope, civilianization, multiskilling, and organizational restructuring.

All key people involved in this contract (the contractor's local manager, the government COR, and most of the workers) worked in the government organization before the A-76 competition. The COR was the functional manager and he contributed substantially to the PWS and MEO development. As a result, we were able to learn much about the use of personnel before and after the A-76 competition through interviews, in spite of the competition being won by a contractor.

The baseline workforce was 52 (23 military, 29 civilian). This baseline already represented a decrease from 75 a few years before, as this competition occurred in the midst of a broader transfer of mission from this installation to others. As a result, we were cautioned that the competition will appear to have generated a lot of personnel savings that actually occurred because of declines in mission.

There were four commercial bids for this contract. The winning contractor bid 23.5 man-years of effort per year. The other contract bids were much higher: 28, 29, and 31 man-years. The MEO bid was 35. Because the winning bid was so much lower, government officials were concerned that this contractor was under-bidding and would not be able to do the work within the bid. However, the technical evaluation team took a special look at the contractor's technical proposal and was ultimately convinced that it could do the work within the bid.

This contractor has several other government contracts for communications functions. The contractor's local manager said that it capitalizes on that experience and transferred lessons learned from other locations to improve efficiency. He also mentioned that this experience is what allowed the contractor to propose the workforce modifications that led to such a low bid.

Multiskilling was a key factor allowing the contractor to perform the function with fewer people. Under the government structure of work, there were two distinct types of workers in the technical control area: operators and technicians. Operators are trained to operate and monitor the machines, while technicians perform maintenance. These jobs are in different federal job series. The technician jobs are more highly paid and require more specialized training. The work also seems to carry a bit more cachet; several of the employees mentioned that technicians tend to view operating tasks as mundane. According to one employee, about 90 percent of the work is operational and only 10 percent maintenance. Operators have to be on site, monitoring and operating the machines around the clock. However, these tasks do not require the full attention of operators; they can do other tasks (such as paper work or repairs) while they perform operator duties.

The contractor determined that the work could be done with far fewer people if they were cross-trained. It hired all of the technicians and trained them as operators (little training was needed, and it occurred informally on the job). It also hired a few operators and has been training them in maintenance, although that is a more involved process because the PWS requires substantial formal training for technicians. According to the contractor's local manager multiskilling alone allowed the contractor to cut eight positions out of the personnel bid. He also noted that the multiskilling allowed the contractor to cut out some supervisory positions. Whereas there used to be an overall supervisor, a maintenance supervisor, and an operations supervisor on each shift, now there is only one supervisor per shift.

Multiskilling has worked out well, although the technicians were reluctant to be cross-trained as operators. One employee reported that the technicians saw it as "demeaning" to perform the operator functions because the work does not require the same level of skills. Another worker noted that technicians are not automatically good operators; they needed time to learn about the circuits, the etiquette involved in operating the different machines, and also just how to operate them. The learning process was not trivial.

Perhaps part of the reason that the workers were not more resistant to the multiskilling is that the contractor ended up paying wages that were between 50 cents and $1 per hour higher than civil service wages—the government workers got a raise when they went to work for the contractor. In spite of this increase, the workforce was unionized within six months of the contract start; wages increased by 10 percent and the workers got more leave. Despite the still-higher wages, the contractor was able to reduce costs by offering fewer benefits than civil service workers received (particularly leave time) and by performing work with fewer people.

Civilianization and organizational streamlining were also important elements of cost saving. The COR noted that civilianization allowed for a substantial amount of savings because, when military people are involved in a particular activity, there is a big "infrastructure" that goes along with it. When this function was performed in-house there was a division officer and several intermediate-level supervisors. For example, under government performance one function was staffed with a training officer, a wiring officer, a division officer, a leading petty officer, and a clerk. The contractor reduced this overhead to one person. The COR also noted that the contractor was able to save on training programs. When the function was performed in-house, people always participated in training programs because the government has a policy of promoting from within. In addition, they faced training requirements through the EEOC to provide advancement opportunities for current workers. The contract has cut training and tried to reduce the cost of training that remains. For example, employees who might move into supervisory positions take supervision courses via CD-ROM.[8]

The contractor's local representative provided another example of savings under the contractor. Formerly, the government organization would detail eight different people for some amount of time each week to clean the building. In addition, there was a contractor providing grounds maintenance. Now, the contractor has one person doing all the cleaning and grass-cutting. That person is doing a better job. According to the COR and the contractor's local representative, this activity presented little opportunity for capital-labor substitution, as this was mainly a service function.

---

[8]While training supervisors via CD-ROM might be less costly, we do not know whether such training is as effective as traditional training.

The PWS changed the scope of work slightly by regionalizing a few relatively small responsibilities: the Defense Information Services Agency (DISA) coordinator functions and the mobile radio test equipment repair and maintenance function.

GOVERNMENT-CONTRACTOR WAGE AND BENEFIT COMPARISONS

PAYING LOWER WAGES AND BENEFITS

In the course of this and a previous competition, we have often heard the argument that contractors provide a service less expensively because they pay lower wages to their workers. For three competitions— AM #2, BOS #2, and MM—we were able to obtain detailed information that allowed us to compare federal wages and benefits for the government positions with the minimum contractor wages and benefits as mandated by the Service Contract Act.[1] For the other competitions, we must rely on anecdotal information about the wage differential. In the tables below, we report the wage plus required fringe benefits (including FICA and Medicare) for comparable occupations[2] and the equivalent minimum for a contractor employee. The government wage rate is the FWS wage rate at step four, or the hourly equivalent of a GS salary at step five.[3] The fringe benefits rate for government employees has been increasing over time. We use whatever rate was in effect at the time the competition

---

[1] We do not have access to information on the actual wages paid by contractors. The DoL wage rate sets a floor on contractor wages and benefits for individual occupations in each local area. Our interviews suggest that because of competitive forces in the contract bidding process, these minimums tend to be binding.

[2] The PWS contains a list of the government positions involved in the function and comparable civilian job titles.

[3] The hourly equivalent for GS employees is calculated by dividing the annual salary by 2087, which is the number of hours of paid full-time work per year.

Table C.2 (continued)

FWS Job Description	FWS Hourly Labor Cost Including Fringe Benefits	DoL Wage Determination	DoL Hourly Labor Cost Including Fringe Benefits
WG-5703-06 motor vehicle operator	$14.77	31290 shuttle bus driver	$12.07
		31300 taxi driver	$11.55
		31361 truck driver, light truck	$12.07
		31362 truck driver, medium truck	$12.67

Table C.3

Government-Contractor Hourly Wage and Benefit Comparison for MM

FWS/GS Job Description	Government Hourly Labor Cost Including Fringe Benefits	DoL Wage Determination	DoL Hourly Labor Cost Including Fringe Benefits
WG-13 electronic integrated systems mechanic	$22.83	23183 electronics technician—maintenance III	$21.84
WG-12 electronic integrated systems mechanic	$21.93	23182 electronics technician—maintenance II	$21.00
GS-07 production control clerk	$18.27	01270 production control clerk	$14.57
GS-05 program specialist clerk	$14.77	01118 general clerk IV	$12.23

difference is consistent with what we were told by those involved in the competition—that the contractor's labor costs would have been about the same as the government's. The government wages for the clerk positions are substantially higher than the DoL wages, but the government benefits costs are much lower. In spite of these slight wage disadvantages, the MEO won this competition. It is worth noting that, in this case, the minimum contractor wages for this competition were substantially higher than the government wages for similar positions, but the contractor's mandated benefits costs were substantially lower.

We were not able to obtain contractor minimum wage information for the other competitions that were won by the in-house organization. However, in BOS #1, the manpower office reported that the contractor's minimum wages were higher than government wages.

We conclude that contractor minimum wages can be but need not be lower than federal wages for equivalent positions.

CONCERNS WITH SAVINGS CALCULATIONS IN A-76 COMPETITIONS

In the course of this analysis, we have identified several limitations in the process used to estimate cost savings in the A-76 competition. We describe these concerns here.

ACTUAL COST MAY DIFFER FROM THE EXPECTED COST

One concern is that the personnel cost estimates are not based on the actual personnel costs associated with the individuals occupying a particular position. Civilian personnel cost estimates include the salary of a GS employee at step five or the annual full-time pay for a step-four FWS worker plus a fringe rate as stipulated in OMB circular A-76. This rate has varied over time and was 32.45 percent in 1996. The baseline estimates we examined did not include other pay,[1] even when other pay was included in the MEO cost estimates. For military personnel, the baseline costs are generally derived from the military standard composite rate for the service in question. This rate includes grade-weighted basic pay, entitlements, and an additional cost for other benefits. The way in which these baseline costs are calculated raises some concerns, but it is not clear that the procedures would lead to an overall overestimate or underestimate of the actual baseline personnel costs. For example, if the workforce has been in place a long time and there is little turnover, the average local step is likely to be above five for GS workers or four for FWS

---

[1]Other pay is compensation to which fringe benefits are not applied. Examples of other pay include overtime pay, night differential, bonuses, and uniform allowances.

workers. In such a situation, the estimates based on wage rates at steps five or four underestimate the actual wage and salary costs. On the other hand, the baseline cost estimates might overestimate actual wage and salary in a function with high turnover where the average step is low. The exclusion of other pay from the calculation will push the estimates down as well, whereas the tendency of installations to include the costs of authorized positions that are not filled will push costs up.

CIVILIANIZATION MAY GENERATE ILLUSORY SAVINGS

Whenever civilianization of military positions is used to reduce the size of the workforce, we believe some of the assumed savings may be illusory. Several managers responsible for developing MEOs told us that they substituted fewer civilian workers (often significantly fewer), for a given number of military workers because military members are often unavailable at their primary duty activity due to training, local details, or deployments. If the training, details, and deployments meet valid and continuing defense requirements, the burden of supporting them is not eliminated by civilianization; rather, it is shifted to other activities with military workforces. However, in A-76 cost calculations, savings that an *activity* realizes by off-loading this burden are not offset by increased costs in other activities to which the burden is shifted.

A different concern is that although military personnel may be removed from the function, the overall number of military authorizations in that service may not decline. In other words, the military authorizations that are deleted from the function are put to use in another activity. Indeed, GAO (NSIAD-99-46, p. 12) reports that although the Army plans to compete about 8000 military positions, it has no plans to reduce military end strength. Instead, it plans to use those personnel to meet other priorities.[2]

_____

[2]This redeployment of military labor may be a good thing for the Army. We simply note the global cost implications of the policy.

MANDATED 12 PERCENT IN-HOUSE OVERHEAD RATE MAY OVERSTATE OVERHEAD COSTS

We note GAO's concern that one factor in the MEO cost calculation, the overhead rate of 12 percent of direct labor costs specified in Circular A-76,[3] lacks an analytical basis and may be overstating or understating the overhead costs associated with in-house performance.[4] According to the GAO, OMB offered DoD and other agencies the opportunity to develop and use another rate, but DoD and the services declined to do so. The 12 percent rate is reportedly a compromise between private-sector interests, which argued for government overhead rates ranging from 15 percent to 30 percent, and rates used in earlier A-76 competitions, which generally ranged from 0 to 3 percent.[5]

This overhead rate is intended to cover two types of overhead. The first is *operations overhead*, defined as those costs that are not 100 percent attributable to the activity, but are generally associated with recurring management and support of the activity. The second is *general and administrative overhead*, including salaries, equipment, space and other activities related to headquarters management, accounting, personnel, legal support, data processing management, and similar common services performed outside the activity.[6]

Although tracing the overhead costs of the activities we studied was beyond the scope of our research, we see indications that the 12 percent rate can misstate the marginal cost of overhead support for in-house performance. In the activities we examined, the cost comparisons were focused on relatively straightforward frontline labor services. Higher-level management services were being retained in-house and were not subject to the MEO or contractor bid. Operations overhead appeared to be undiminished by outsourcing. Outsourcing did not reduce command, executive, and functional

---

[3]U.S. Office of Management and Budget, *Circular No. A-76, Revised Supplemental Handbook*, Mar. 1996, p. 23.

[4]GAO, *Defense Outsourcing: Better Data Needed to Support Overhead Rates for A-76 Studies*, GAO/NSIAD-98-62, Feb. 1998, p. 12.

[5]GAO, 1998, pp. 4–6.

[6]OMB, p. 23.

oversight responsibilities at higher organizational levels (installation, major command, or service headquarters). Further, because contractors occupied government-furnished facilities and used government-furnished equipment and parts, large pieces of general and administrative overhead were also common to in-house and contractor performance. The only significant overhead costs we believe were saved through these competitions are those associated with personnel and payroll support of the displaced civil service workforce (due to a reduction in MEO staffing or outsourcing).

We do not know what the appropriate overhead rate might be for these six competitions. However, we note that personnel-related occupations occupy only 1.75 percent of the DoD workforce.[7] The salaries of the staffs of local and regional civilian personnel offices and headquarters functions probably constitute the largest element of the overhead rate. As a proportion of direct labor cost of an activity, the average overhead cost is unlikely to be much greater than the ratio of personnel specialists to personnel. The marginal rate would be less than the average rate. As a result, we believe it likely that MEO costs were substantially overstated in the competitions we examined. If true, this overstatement resulted in inflated costs for the MEOs and inflated savings estimates (relative to the MEO) for those activities that were outsourced.

The 12 percent rule might also understate the overhead cost savings, particularly in cases where the PWS requires the contractor or MEO to assume a substantial amount of work management, facilities management, supply functions, discretion over work processes, and broad accountability for program outcomes. If the DoD outsources larger and more complex activities and concurrently reduces its management and oversight of production processes, then greater overhead cost savings may be attainable.

Currently, what the overhead personnel costs should capture is not well understood, and it is likely that the potential incremental overhead cost savings in the event of outsourcing or a more streamlined MEO vary dramatically by competition. Before the introduction of

---

[7]Data derived from U.S. Office of Personnel Management, *Federal Civilian Workforce Statistics: Occupations of Federal White-Collar and Blue-Collar Workers as of September 30, 1997*, OMSOE-OWI-56-25, September 1998.

the 12 percent rule, most DoD competitions did not include any such overhead cost in the in-house bid. Clearly, some overhead cost should be applied to the in-house bid. However, we believe that the imposition of an arbitrary 12 percent rate does not appropriately capture the costs and therefore reduces the credibility of the cost-comparison process. Therefore, we believe this issue warrants further study.

Baldwin, Laura H., Frank Camm, Edward G. Keating, and Ellen M. Pint, *Incentives to Undertake Sourcing Studies in the Air Force.* Santa Monica, Calif.: RAND, DB-240-AF, 1998.

Commission on Roles and Missions of the Armed Forces, Directions for Defense, Washington, D.C., May 24, 1995.

Gates, Susan M., and Albert A. Robbert, *Comparing the Costs of DoD Military and Civil Service Personnel.* Santa Monica, Calif.: RAND, MR-980-OSD, 1998.

General Accounting Office, *DOD Competitive Sourcing: Questions About Goals, Pace, and Risks of key Reform Initiative.* Washington, D.C.: GAO/NSIAD-99-46, February 1999.

General Accounting Office, *DOD Competitive Sourcing: Results of Recent Competitions.* Washington, D.C.: GAO/NSIAD-99-44, February 1999.

General Accounting Office, *Future Years Defense Program: How Savings from Reform Initiatives Affect DOD's 1999–2003 Program.* Washington, D.C.: GAO/NSIAD-99-66, February 1999.

General Accounting Office, *Defense Outsourcing: Better Data Needed to Support Overhead Rates for A-76 Studies.* Washington, D.C.: GAO/NSIAD-98-62, February 1998.

General Accounting Office, *Future Years Defense Program: Substantial Risks Remain in DOD's 1999–2003 Plan.* Washington, D.C.: GAO/NSIAD-98-204, July 1998.

General Accounting Office, *Federal Management: Serious Management Problems Facing Major Agencies.* Washington, D.C.: GAO/OCG-98-1R, October 1997.

General Accounting Office, *Defense Infrastructure: Costs Projected to Increase Between 1997 and 2001.* Washington, D.C.: GAO/NSIAD-96-174, May 1996.

General Accounting Office, *Defense Infrastructure: Challenges Facing DoD In Implementing Reform Initiatives.* Washington, D.C.: GAO/NSIAD-96-115, March 1996.

General Accounting Office, *Defense Infrastructure: Budget Estimates for 1996-2001 Offer Little Savings for Modernization.* Washington, D.C.: GAO/NSIAD-96-131, April 1996.

General Accounting Office, *DoD Functions Contracted Out Under OMB Circular A-76: Contract Cost Increases And the Effects on Federal Employees.* Washington, D.C.: GAO/NSIAD-85-49, April 1985.

General Accounting Office, *OMB Circular A-76: Expected Savings Are Not Being Realized in Ft. Sill's Logistics Contract.* Washington, D.C.: GAO/GGD-91-33, February 1991.

General Accounting Office, *OMB Circular A-76: DoD's Reported Savings Figures Are Incomplete and Inaccurate.* Washington, D.C.: GAO/GGD-90-58, March 1990.

Handy, John B., and Dennis J. O'Conner, *How Winners Win: Lessons Learned from Contract Competitions in Base Operations Support*, Bethesda, Md.: Logistics Management Institute, 1984.

Keating, Edward G., *Cancellations and Delays in Completion of Department of Defense A-76 Cost Comparisons.* Santa Monica, Calif.: RAND, DB-191-OSD, 1997.

Moore, Nancy Y., Rick Eden, and Mark Wang. *USMC Sourcing Competitions: One Approach for Lowering Costs and Improving Performance.* Santa Monica, Calif.: RAND, DB-250-USMC, 1998.

Niskanen, W. A., Jr., *Bureaucracy and Representative Government*, Chicago: Aldine, 1971.

Office of Management and Budget, "Performance of Commercial Activities," Circular No. A-76, Revised Supplemental Handbook, March 1996.

Robbert, Albert A., Susan M. Gates, and Marc N. Elliott, *Outsourcing of DoD Commercial Activities: Impacts on Civil Service Employees*. Santa Monica, Calif.: RAND, MR-866-OSD, 1997.

Snyder, Christopher M., Robert P. Trost, and R. Derek Trunkey, *Bidding Behavior in DoD's Commercial Activities Competitions*. Alexandria, Va.: Center for Naval Analysis, CRM 97-68, January 1998.

Tighe, Carla E., Samuel D. Kleinman, James M. Jondrow, and R. Derek Trunkey, *Outsourcing and Competition: Lessons Learned from DOD Commercial Activities Programs*. Alexandria, Va.: Center for Naval Analysis, Occasional Paper, October 1996.

Trunkey, R. Derek et al., *Moving Forward with A-76 in the Navy*. Alexandria, Va.: Center for Naval Analysis, CRM 98-9, April 1998.

Paulson, Robert M., and Arnold Zimmer, *An Analysis of Methods of Base Support: Contractor Operations Versus Standard Operations at Two Undergraduate Pilot Training Bases*. Santa Monica, Calif.: RAND, R-1563-PR, 1975.

Shishko, Robert, Robert M. Paulson, and Wayne D. Perry, *Alternative Methods for Base Support Operations at Undergraduate Pilot Training Bases: An Update*. Santa Monica, Calif.: RAND, R-2181-MRAL, 1977.

Yim, Randall A., "Revisions to the Commercial Activities Management Information System (CAMIS) Procedural Guidance," Memorandum, Office of the Under Secretary of Defense for Acquisition and Technology to the Secretaries of the Military Departments and the Directors of the Defense Logistics Agency, the Defense Finance and Accounting System, and the Defense Commissary Agency, September 3, 1999.